MAC 'N CHEESE

Mini morsels for positive performance

MAC 'N CHEESE

MINI MORSELS FOR POSITIVE PERFORMANCE

By

Marilyn Gansel, PsyD

Copyright © 2018 Marilyn Gansel, PsyD

Publishing Services by Happy Self Publishing
www.happyselfpublishing.com

Year: 2018

All rights reserved. No reproduction, transmission or copy of this publication can be made without the written consent of the author in accordance with the provision of the Copyright Acts. Any person doing so will be liable to civil claims and criminal prosecution.

Dedicated

To Torie

*For her love, friendship **and** her mac 'n cheese*

You may be asking *why* **this** title for a book?

I never *liked* mac 'n cheese casseroles. Perhaps that's because the ones I was familiar with, were store bought. Now there is nothing wrong with pre-packaged food, but the mac 'n cheeses I have tasted just weren't that great... nothing to rave about...or even worth a 5 star review.

Until my friend Torie baked mac 'n cheese casseroles at every holiday gathering. I was hooked! Now, I understand readers who are chefs, who like to cook, and those who just want to know...what the SECRET ingredient is! What makes her mac 'n cheese so scrumptious?

What is the recipe?

Torie doesn't have just one recipe that she follows. She creatively changes ingredients. So the taste varies each time. However, the casseroles are delectable. Her mac 'n cheese sustains us.

Why is Torie's mac 'n cheese so nurturing? Mac 'n cheese is known as comfort food. It is a dish that typically appears around the holidays. This casserole somehow makes us feel connected to one another. Each mac is tightly arranged side by side, swimming in the melted cheese. Torie's mac 'n cheese is held together by one essential ingredient **–her love** baked in a long with the recipe's ever changing add-ons. Whatever ingredient is in the recipe does not matter; we slowly savor each morsel of macaroni bathed in liquefied cheese. We chew with contentment; often refilling our plates for more. When we reach our limit, we push away from the table, laughing at our consumption of so much mac 'n cheese. Then, we really converse; because that's what a gathering around food is—an exchange among friends, about topics that really resonate with us.

We swap stories about life and the lessons learned... the good, the bad, and the ugly. Our conversations range from topic to topic—from history to art, travel, children, grandchildren, and even to personal growth and development. They include personal life struggles from divorce to dating, career to entrepreneurial endeavors, politics to the daily challenges and how to perform more positively at work, home, and play. We discuss what is truly meaningful and purposeful in our lives like our community, world, what really matters; and, in the heated moments of enthusiasm, we all talk at the same time—a cacophony of harmony and passion.

Torie's mac' n cheese binds us together as we eat, talk, and search for our life's purpose. In an attempt to make meaning out of life's ups and downs, we share tidbits of wisdom that keep us exploring, expanding, and evolving into who we are becoming—*positive performers*.

Table of Content

Preface

This book is my dish of mac 'n cheese written by me to you, with love. Each chapter is the short-length macaroni in Torie's casserole. EACH POST IS THE BREAD CRUMB CRUST. DIG IN AND TAKE A BITE. EXPLORE NEW TASTES AND TERRITORIES; EXPAND YOUR HORIZONS AND EVOLVE INTO WHO YOU ARE BECOMING. My recipe for mac 'n cheese is a compilation of wisdom gathered over time—heated in the oven of my life—cooked over time for a positive performance at home, at play and work.

Here is an opportunity for you to optimize your performance, become more resilient, confident, and optimistic. As you dig into this book, you will uncover simple methods to change, grow, and function more positively. Whoever you are, wherever you are at this moment, in whatever career you are in or are pursuing. You will take away little bits of wisdom as a leader, manager, counselor, family members, an employee, or even as a member of a team. You will be challenged to incorporate mental strategies daily, identifying unconscious patterns of resistance. You will be instructed to move out of your comfort zone-- employing positive tactics to help with **over thinking and negative thinking,** which clearly sabotages your best performance.

You will be encouraged to see life's challenges as opportunities for growth. You will find practical applications to move from your current mindset towards a more introspective, growth-producing fruitful, happier one. In other words, you will move from a fixed mindset towards a growth mindset. You will explore, expand, and evolve into you. You will build a foundation based on your strengths and values. You will be inspired to remove limiting beliefs and to take action. You will see your obstacles from a different perspective. Let that outlook allow you to grow and perform better.

> "The thing that is really hard, and really amazing, is giving up on being perfect and beginning the work of becoming yourself."

Dig into my mac' n cheese; however, like Torie says, "Leave room for dessert!"

⬥━━━━⬥

Driven to Perfection

I am DTP (driven to perfection.) That is the best way to describe me.

I didn't think I was a duty-bound person; but, in my mid-thirties, my pastor asked me why I was so driven! I didn't consider myself obsessed. I pictured myself as ambitious, energetic, focused, and motivated to be successful. That inner drive to succeed propelled me to constantly take on new challenges and embark on novel projects. So, I took my pastor's question about being driven to be a positive comment. After all, my ambition was a value that aligned with whom I was becoming.

However, I am recently evaluating my life. Have I have been trying to prove that I am just as good as the next person just as smart, just as pretty, just as loveable, and just as perfect as the world wants me? I have been asking myself where this *driven* quality came from. It seems to be engrained in my core being; and I believe it stems from several things that my mother said to me when I was a child.

"I never wanted you," my mother told me one day as she was brushing my hair. I must have been around three or four at the time. "I never wanted you. When I found out I was pregnant, I went to the doctor and asked him to remove the baby by using a coat hanger, or whatever. But I'm glad I have you. In the end, I'm glad."

You never forget when someone says "I never wanted you" even if they follow it with "but" and attempt to qualify what they mean. Those words, imprinted in my subconscious, fueled the way I saw myself throughout my life: unworthy, less than perfect, a reject; someone who could be tossed aside for someone more valuable or more loveable.

Perhaps my mother felt unworthy too. She was raised with eight brothers and sisters; all the boys slept in one bed, the girls in another. My grandmother took potato sacks and bleached them to sew undergarments for the family. My grandparents spoke in broken English. So at an early age, my mother suggested that I *surround myself with people better than me*. Not that it was a bad thing for her to say. She and my dad did not have the opportunity to finish high school or grammar school. They had to find jobs as soon as they could, in order to help their parents. However, surrounding me with people who were better than me, may have contributed to the low self-esteem I already had. We were poor and I began finding friends out of my league, classmates who led privileged lives. I didn't have the experiences that they had, allowances, travel, or the culture. My upbringing was simple and unsophisticated. I knew early on that I didn't belong in that circle; but I pretended to. I tried so hard in my driven way to be perfect.

I had terrible learning problems as a child. I was always failing in school. Teachers told me that I wouldn't amount to much. And I believed that story for a while. I became silent and shy, unable to voice an opinion. It didn't help either that at home, as a female my words didn't count, my desires to obtain an education beyond high school didn't matter. I would be married and have children and stay home. No one asked me what I wanted. Inside, I wanted to prove everyone wrong.

And then, after high school, it hit me. I had to leave home. I had to get into a college. I needed to push myself and prove to the world that I wasn't unworthy or dumb. I didn't want people to find out that I was less than perfect.

So I hid behind the mask of perfection driving myself to illness, depression, and anxiety. I would appear smart, witty, worthy, and perfectly successful. Yet, all the while, I felt unsure, unsafe, unworthy, and uncertain. I had to drive myself harder to prove that I am loved.

Today, I can say that while these feelings are still within me, rising up to the surface every now and then, I am more content with the story of me. Yes, perfection is part of my character. My drive to prove is still showing up. But I am more mindful of where those personality traits came from. Without judgment, I know that I am never going to be perfect and that is all right. I am still worthy and loved. I can ease up on the driven nature of who I am. I can begin to relax and see that in the eyes of the one who created me, I am **enough**.

I am enough for today; there is a tomorrow.

Mini Morsel Sampling

What does perfection mean to you? What is driving you? Is there any correlation to what drove you earlier in life? What steps can you take to be less perfect, less driven? What would have to happen for you to believe that you are enough?

Thoughts Become Things: Changing Externally by Shifting Internally

Have you ever wondered what it would be like to shape shift? Morph into some creature that you would like to be? Change instantaneously, without the slightest hesitation, at any given moment. You could create an appearance of your choosing. What do you want to look like? Or, better yet, who do you want to look like?

> "If you see it in your mind, you will see it in your hand."
> Don Proctor

Perhaps, as our society relies on cosmetic surgery to transform our smallest flaw, to shape shift our bodies into our perception of perfection, we are moving toward shape shifting.

I know that we are obsessed with changing externally. Look what we do to make ourselves attractive, popular, and even seen as successful! Dare we look different? I think we are getting away from the dissimilarities and morphing into what we think is acceptable, beautiful, and pleasurable. There was a time when body piercing and tattooing were thought to be vulgar, they are now considered as the norm. Now, I am not saying that body art shouldn't be applied. I am just curious as to why we are so focused on external beauty when internal beauty is rarely cultivated.

I would ask you to spend some time admiring your inner beauty. Be patient with yourself. Show compassion to yourself. Engage in positive self-talk, adopt an attitude with gratitude, a sense of humor and focus on the attributes that make you the person you are becoming. Look at your soul, and your heart. Listen to what your heart is really telling you. Believe your gut not what others are saying or what you believe as the truth. Really search and dig deep. I bet if you tend to your inner beauty, like a garden, your external beauty will be extremely striking. You may find that life takes a different shift attracting new friends, sharing new possibilities. Celebrate your inner beauty. Unleash it! Let it do its thing. You will be amazed at its power.

"The beauty of a woman is not in the clothes she wears, the figure that she carries, or the way she combs her hair.

The beauty of a woman is seen in her eyes, because that is the doorway to her heart, the place where love resides. True beauty in a woman is reflected in her soul. It's the caring that she lovingly gives the passion that she shows & the beauty of a woman only grows with passing years."

-Audrey Hepburn

Mini Morsel Sampling:

Look in the mirror; focus on what you love about yourself. Your smile? Your hair? Your eyes? Your personality? What is it about the inner you that makes people feel drawn to you? If you don't know, then ask someone you trust. Then tend to that inner part of you that makes you unique and you will discover an attractiveness that is beyond just the physical.

Did anyone ever tell you to do something and that it would build your character?

I can remember numerous occasions when adults had me do something I hated but they

"Sports do not build character. They reveal it."
Heywood Broun

assured me saying it would build my character. I suppose that I gained a good foundation in character building—often, it seemed like I was swallowing my pride, being humble, and accepting menial tasks all in pursuit of this new emerging me!

But now, I realize in life and especially in sports, that the games we play do not build character. They reveal it. They reveal who we really are deep down like when we are up against moral and ethical decisions, what do we choose to do? Do we dig deep inside ourselves and call up the true fiber of who we are? Do we stand firm in our commitments or do we shakily move further from the truth of our foundations? Do we act to prevent atrocities? Or do we allow the violent and cruel deeds of others to continue?

I wonder if we as a society have forgotten that character traits—the distinguishing marks that tell us whether a person has a strong character—are crucial for leadership. Whether in the political or sports arena these traits are important for society to thrive.

It's easy in sports (and in life) to forget or not have learned the qualities that show a person could be of a high moral character. It's easy to forget the character building blocks of resiliency, responsibility, confidence, gratitude, respect, compassion, integrity, patience, sportsmanship, and empathy. But I do believe that today more than ever we need to learn to build character by incorporating these traits and values into our daily teachings.

In an ideal world, your family may have taught you love, and then the courage of conviction, compassion, respect, responsibility, integrity, honesty. Maybe you were lucky enough to have gotten through the entire character trait table. In our less-than-ideal world, you can still do your best and practice at least six character traits. Master them and share them.

Character must be cultivated; it takes practice to make responsible choices about how we do things, not just about what we do.

Mini Morsel Sampling:

Focus on six character traits that you would like to develop. Circle them below. Write them on a post-it and view them as if they have already happened...that they are a part of who you are. In two weeks, write what you learned about yourself as you are integrating these traits into your daily life.

Positive Character Traits

kind	reliable	easygoing
generous	energetic	creative
enthusiastic	upbeat	considerate
responsible	understanding	thoughtful
brave	confident	artistic
honest	observant	cooperative
hard working	compassionate	cheerful
imaginitive	insightful	motivated
intelligent	witty	courageous
trustworthy	flexible	open-minded
optimistic	supportive	patient
unselfish	organized	reasonable
considerate	determined	outgoing
helpful	humorous	independent
encouraging	respectful	articulate
polite	caring	dedicated
careful	empathetic	focused
ambitious	forgiving	generous
modest	persistent	quiet
reliable	sincere	thorough
clever	accepting	positive

MINI MORSEL 3

If you can dream it, you can do it.

In the silent stillness, I hear wisdom speaking
Awakening my sleepy inner self
Coaxing me to explore, discover and pursue
The authentic, magical, spiritual me
My journey's path much traveled led me
To experiences unwanted at times, but so necessary for growth

In the silent stillness, wisdom is urging me to face life
With courage, determination, and resiliency
To take avenues untraveled with desire, vision, and persistence
To choose confidence, erasing fear and nagging doubt
My mental acuity is heightened bringing me to
The person I am meant to be now...the dreams today I hold sacred...

> "If you can dream it, you can do it."
> Walt Disney

The hope for meaning as I listen to wisdom in the stillness of silence

> ***Mini Morsel Sampling:***
>
> *Meditation for some people is just hard. The mind wanders constantly and attempting to focus on one thing becomes almost painful. But I have discovered that walking meditation works...at least for me. As you go about your day, welcome moments of silence and just be. If you cannot sit and meditate, then walk in quiet peacefulness and find one to two things for which you are grateful. Stay with these appreciative thoughts for five minutes increasing to a comfortable length of time during your day.*

Dreams

You have exactly what it takes to make your dreams come true.

You have exactly what it takes

- to start a business
- to be a parent
- to run a marathon
- to climb a mountain
- to change careers
- to improve relationships

- to mend a broken promise
- to create a new product
- to get the job done
- to leave a legacy
- to push peace not war
- to address discrimination
- to change the world a day at a time

So, why aren't you doing it? You have exactly what it takes. You just have to believe and then **act** on it. Don't depend on others to make your dreams come true. It all starts with you and me.

Mini Morsel Sampling:

What are your immediate dreams? What are your future dreams? What do you need to do to make them happen? Do you need other resources? People? Places? Education? Research? Outline small weekly steps that you can take that will help you act each and every day.

Wishing for something is probably the first thing I do when I want something to happen. However, I noticed recently that just wishing, is not bringing me results. Growing wishbones without goals, drive, and purpose just amounts to the

"Never grow a wishbone, daughter, where you backbone ought to be"—

Clementine Paddleford

bones accumulating in my closet. I realize that I have to take the wishes or dreams out of the closet and then turn them into backbones. I am in the process of rearranging my wishbones and fashioning them into a strong, empowered backbone that is ready to take on the world. It's not easy. My bones don't always line up the way I think they should, in order to form my powerful, inspiring backbone. But I am working on creating one that will help me wish mindfully and not thoughtlessly. Sure, I could wish for the frivolous. I could wish for luxuries–and that's OK to do that. I want to wish for things like leaving a legacy or helping others. So, that takes a backbone not just a wishbone. I will keep wishing for all sorts of things (because we are meant to dream) but I will do more selective wishing; with more courage and conviction visualizing my wishes into realities.

Oh, and I plan to grow some funny bones too. Because, I need a sense of humor especially when my wishes don't come true (and maybe that is a good thing) or when my backbone bends a bit and just doesn't give me what I think I want. So I am going to choose to bend a bit, be more flexible, and let my backbone do what it can provided the time and resources I have are available. I will use my sense of humor and the spirit of play to gather up my wishes and erect the backbone I need, to leave behind a legacy and to help others. And I will definitely need laughter especially when I feel challenged.

Mini Morsel Sampling:

So, what are your wishes? First, look at a picture of a human backbone. There are thirty-three vertebrae in the human backbone. Write down numbers one to thirty-three on a piece of paper. At the coccyx, write your dream or find a picture of your dream and place it at the bottom of your spine. Now create your wish backbone by writing actions that take you to the top of the cervix that making your wish come true. Make sure you visit your backbone daily and add some funny bones along the way, when you have a setback. Laugh at yourself when you climb the wish backbone; we all fall short at times.

"The most vital thing in a man's life is his mental attitude."

Mental Attitude: Behind the Smile

This came to me by email. I thought about this writer's opinion and wasn't going to comment except I just feel misunderstood.

"Dr. Marilyn: While I admire your energy, optimism, and ambition… I find your approach to human health disturbing. It seems to be based on a typically American, somewhat overly commercial, everyone-should-always-be-optimistic point of view. My question to you is: do you ever entertain any doubts? Frankly, the way you advertise your business and yourself– the big smile, etc. leads me to distrust your approach. Have you ever considered that your approach isn't quite so perfect, and does some harm as well as good?"

To the writer of this email and all others who doubt the *authentic me*, let me tell you what is behind my *big* smile.

My big smile reflects who I am becoming: someone who is trying to love unconditionally and someone who wishes to bring brightness to a world that is struggling. My smile is the first thing people see, which I hope is warm and welcoming. I see many unhappy, unsmiling American people. Maybe that's in my line of business. I see sad, dissatisfied, unfulfilled Americans looking for ways to alleviate, soothe, and fill up their emptiness. And, many times, they do it in very destructive ways.

I guess my wide smile in my advertising photo confuses you. I cannot apologize for that. I cannot plaster a miserable, dejected face on my website or in my advertising to convince you that I am like you–a real person with real problems. Instead I choose to show my smile which (hopefully) radiates joy and happiness even when my life isn't so perfect; because, you see, it never has been perfect. My smile doesn't show my pain or sorrow, my doubts or fears; but let me tell you, I have had them and still have. I know loss. I lost my best friend to suicide. I lost 5 family members in two and a half years. I know uncertainty. Most of my life, I have feared the unknown–would I pass my classes in school? Would I find love? Would I find a fulfilling job? Would I be the best? I was always the last to be chosen for anything. I know fear—fear of flying, fear of public speaking, fear of being put down, or fear of being ridiculed about my beliefs. I know depression. I suffered for years feeling like I wouldn't amount to anything. I had and still fight the limiting beliefs that can hold me back. I have hated the way I looked. I too struggle with low self-esteem.

I smile because I choose to, because it is my gift to the people I meet. When my husband had cancer and an open heart surgery, I went to work each day with a smile. When I opened the door to that job, I left my pain and sadness behind because I was needed as a teacher (my career then) and as a positive performance coach (my career now). My students needed me. My clients need me. Sometimes I would go out to my car at lunch and cry when my husband was ill; but I would return smiling because, as my aunt used to say "What's the use of complaining?" When my dad was dying from pancreatic and colon cancer, he still smiled and still was grateful. I choose the 'attitude with gratitude' approach. I want my smile to bring hope and encouragement. We need optimistic people to bolster our spirits. We need inspiration!

I know you cannot see me behind my smile. Just know that perhaps if you got to know me, you would know that the cover is not what is in the book. It's got depth and breath. I'm just a woman wishing better things for the world.

> **Mini Morsel Sampling:**
>
> *What new small steps can you take today to help you stay positive, happy, and optimistic at work, home or play without appearing unauthentic? Make sure the steps you take are bringing you a smile. Not forced but genuinely happy.*

Has anyone told you that you are such a strong person? Or that your resiliency is a strength that they wish they had?

What's your inner YOU showing on the outside to the public?

I have been told over and over
again that I am a feisty, resilient person. I have been asked about where I get my boundless energy, why I am thoughtful or grateful, and how I sustain my limitless fortitude.

Like, Robin Williams who committed suicide; I understand the depths of depression and anxiety. Many people endure with great stamina and courage, struggles that no one knows about. Often we are silent; why would anyone want to know about our feelings, our doubts, and our insecurities? Most people want to escape, to laugh, to remove themselves from disturbing thoughts and painful memories.

Perhaps that is why people like Robin Williams enjoy seeing people laugh, being an entertainer, and creating a picture of ourselves quite different to what is happening internally. It may be how we get through our day—outwardly joyful, confident, and buoyant.

I used to be so quiet about my depression. I felt that it stigmatized me; but recently I began to tell others about what is happening. I began to share my deepest, saddest thoughts, and my most vivid reflections of my life, its meaning and purpose. I went public. And it felt right because I found out that I am not alone.

I have been strong enough far too long; perhaps you too have been strong for too long. It is time to come together and say "You can share. I will listen. I understand. I have been there." You can offer encouragement so that you and others like me will bounce back, in time. A tidbit of advice: surround yourself with supportive people. Remember you are not alone. When you feel like the whole world around you is collapsing, remember that you can build yourself up—one day at a time—find the time to renew, recharge, and not quit. There is a purpose here. I know that. Look for your purpose.

> ### *Mini Morsel Sampling:*
>
> *We would not be human if we did not experience tough times. We all feel vulnerable from time to time. We feel that life is at times unfair. We find great moments of sadness BUT we can learn from anxiety, fear, and depression. We can support each other; create new stories of ourselves; and, be confident. Find 2 people who can support you in times when you need to be heard, not judged but listened to, not criticized for your feelings but praised for your insight and willingness to grow from the experience. Look for your purpose.*

MINI MORSEL 5

❖

"If you want more kindness in the world, put it there."

Pay it forward

"**U**ntil you change the way you live your life, life as you know it, will never change! Make a difference that matters, pay it forward daily"

Have you ever been faced with a challenge and wondered "why is this happening to me?"

Change starts internally—within me, and then I focus on external changes.

I have had to look at the way I lived my life and transform it. For example, in my thirties I was overweight, asthmatic, and depressed. I also suffered from extreme back pain. On medicine for depression, I hoped for relief from my *out of control* life. But the medicine did not provide the cure I sought. The cure came from a little voice inside me that told me I had to make some difficult, dramatic, and daring decisions in my life.

At that time, instead of moving forward and listening to that voice, I chose to remain in a joyless job. I worked constantly striving to achieve and acquire more things. I stayed there for ten more years until one day, my husband got cancer. I realized through his pain that my own pain was just as cancerous as his—what I was doing was wasting my time.

So, I quit the job that was then giving me little fulfillment. I chose to listen to my gut, to quiet my mind, and to move from fear to victory. I opened my own business and started living my life as an entrepreneur. I used all my skills and knowledge from my previous career to hone a successful business. But now I could do things on my own terms and be a creative, innovative marketer. I could write more and present at seminars. I could become more confident and become the host of my own radio show, "What's Weighing You Down?" on www.FTNS.co for two years.

I made a difference to others in my former career and I know I paid it forward as well. But in my new business, I felt that I could make even more of a difference. Each day I went to work, it felt like *play*. It was so pleasurable. I met the most amazing people—who wouldn't want to pay it forward?

"We can do it!"

One week on my internet radio show, I interviewed a remarkable woman—Jessica Scofield. She is now the nation's best female power lifter. Globally, she is ranked fourth. She competes in an arena where men have dominated. We talked about empowering women on my show. As we talked, I was reminded of another incredible and empowered woman, my aunt Elbina. She also gave to people without expecting anything in return.

My aunt Elbina operated our family furniture and moving business along with her four brothers at a time when women rarely held prominent business positions. She cemented the success of that business. Her mother and father, immigrants from Italy, spoke broken English. But her dad, Pellegrino, was astutely aware that to get ahead, he would have to purchase properties in his new home town in America and open several businesses. His most successful entrepreneurial venture, the furniture and moving company, was unfortunately cut short by his untimely death. He was hit by a bus and instantly died.

Elbina, a graduate of the Merrill Business School and the New York School of Interior Decorating seized the opportunity to work with her brothers and make the business a huge success, prospering for sixty years!

My aunt worked long hard hours. She used to say, "What's the use of complaining?" Why bother to complain–just do it! (Nike would have loved to hear her use their tag line well before they did). She endured two failed marriages, took care of her mother (who lived with my aunt), and had no children–just a little dog. After long days at the office, she would come home sometimes at 9 p.m. to have a quick dinner and soak her aching feet in a basin of warm water. Elbina traveled and spent time volunteering. At the family business, people gravitated to her; her smile was genuine. She gave little gifts to her patrons–a lamp for their room, a small thought for their child. She was extremely generous. At Christmas, all the nieces and nephews would receive a Christmas club check; that check was a result of my aunt depositing a few dollars for each of us in a special account so that at Christmas we would be able to purchase something we wanted.

Elbina valued education; so, when I longed to go to college and did not have the money, Elbina paid for my tuition. I didn't mind working as a waitress in college to supplement her gift to me. I wanted to be like her–strong, courageous, and determined to succeed in spite of hardships.

When my aunt took ill and her ovarian cancer seemed to eat away at her, she still never complained. She continued to roll up her sleeves and do whatever needed to be done at work and at home. Towards the end of her life, she told me that she didn't fear death. She lived her life. It was full. It didn't seem full to me; but, Elbina was satisfied. Nursing her mother as she lay dying, struggling with her own cancer battle, Elbina exhibited love and patience–never really focusing on herself.

Now, as I look back on where I have been and where I am going, I am thankful to have had such a wonderful role model in my aunt Elbina. She was a woman far ahead of her time. She succeeded in the market place where men thrived and women hardly chose to go. She was an empowered woman. And she empowered me. She instilled the **we can do it** attitude in me.

Mini Morsel Sampling:

What can you do this week to be more empowered?
And how can you pay it forward?

Got Purpose?

Do you have it? And do you know what that purpose is?

Sometimes your purpose may change direction but not its intention!

When I was a child, I felt like I was called to serve others. At first, I was interested in serving by teaching youngsters because I witnessed the value of education. My mother had to work after eighth grade; and my dad lost his father at a young age and had to work in the family business. Dad only made it to sixth grade. They never enjoyed literature, read history books, or expressed their own thoughts in eloquent style.

Both sets of grandparents emigrated from Italy and could not read or write in English; I often accompanied by Grandmother Longo (Angelina) down West Avenue in Stamford, CT to her reading/grammar classes. I watched her struggle with the language but her steadfastness made me more determined than ever to seek knowledge through learning.

I was also intrigued by social work but my deepest desire was to be an actress— to be part of a theatrical company.

Subconsciously, perhaps I took those things I loved and the talents I had and used them for a life of purpose—

serving in ways that at first seemed unrelated but now seem very connected and meaningful.

So, when I think about my purpose—my reason for being here—my calling as a teacher, media specialist, wife, mother, entrepreneur, fitness expert, sports psychologist, vitamin/beauty consultant, writer and radio host, I see that my purpose never changed—just the direction in which I would serve.

I could inspire and minister in my life—through joy and sorrow because that is what I was meant to do—take meaning and opportunity from every encounter and learn. I intentionally chose (or maybe it was chosen for me) to experience all I have to give back to others what I uncovered and now know.

Some individuals do not know their purpose or think they have one but exploring and discovering what it is you are meant to do at any stage of your life—even in retirement—is a real adventure. It instills in me a sense of curiosity; for, I believe, when you stop being curious, you avoid possibilities. Who knows what lies ahead?

I never knew that my journey would take me on exploits where I would meet the most amazing people in my life— whose narratives impacted me greatly. Over the past two years, I have spoken with individuals whose lives were touched by pain, purpose, and passion. And those stories developed into a book of twenty-two inspirational and compelling short stories that is now available on amazon.com.

It is fittingly titled: "Pain, Purpose, Passion: That Was Then, This Is Now."

I hope that you will read this book (my own short story is included) and be inspired to find your purpose wherever you are right now.

> ***Mini Morsel Sampling:***
>
> *Got purpose? Be curious! Map the places you've experienced whether it is work, school, and/or pleasure. See the connections in your life journey. What similarities and differences do you notice? Be mindful of them as you further explore and expand your life's path.*

It's not about you!

Listening to Charles Osgood on television, I was mesmerized by his segment about a young man named Jeff Hanson.

"The welfare of each is bound up in the welfare of all."—Helen Keller

In case you haven't heard of him, Jeff is a philanthropic artist from Overland Park, Kansas. He is visually impaired from an optic nerve tumor (he nicknamed CLOD) associated with a genetic condition called neurofibromatosis. The tumor caused severe vision loss in 2005, requiring chemotherapy and radiation. Despite his low vision, Jeff sees well enough to continue creating brilliant artwork.

What really enticed me to watch this piece was its title: Inner Vision. Jeff has that inner ability to see life in its spectacular form—painting bold, colorful masterpieces that sell sometimes at a very high price. But Jeff isn't in this for the money. He is in it to make change happen— one painting at a time!

Jeff could have had his tumor, chemotherapy and radiation therapy cloud his vision on life. But he didn't let that happen.

Instead, his inner vision created awareness that *it's not about you…it's about others*. For Jeff sees with his heart and gives abundantly to charities. He is a true testament to Helen Keller's philosophy that *the welfare of each is bound up in the welfare of all*.

Jeff has learned lessons from which we can all benefit: "Live life with a purpose. Don't let your illness define you. Generosity begets generosity. Be passionate in everything you do." And he is. Donating more than a million dollars in acrylic canvases to over hundred charities worldwide since 2006, Jeff amazingly raised this amount by the age of twenty!

His mission of compassion as an artist, entrepreneur, and philanthropist makes me wonder about my own inner vision. I have my eyesight yet sometimes I don't act on my inner vision. I am often blinded by adversities instead of choosing to use hardships as opportunities. This story was truly an eye-opener.

I hope that you too will consider listening to your heart and seeing with your inner vision.

Mini Morsel Sampling:

Focus today on your inner vision. Close your eyes. Picture yourself giving to others; then act on it. You will be surprised; you will see the world differently and in the end, see yourself open to purpose.

Grief "It doesn't get better, it gets different."

I know grief all too well. I've lost five family members within two and a half years. Recently, my mom died.

I remember in college losing my grandfather and that death devastated me. He always called me *Nina*. It was an affectionate term of endearment. It warmed my heart to be near this lovely man who grew up in Italy and whose occupation was shepherding and farming. I always pictured him on the hills in his home town quietly tending his flock. He was tender and loving; it broke my heart when he died.

It seemed as if after college one by one my family members developed diabetes, cancer, or suffered massive heart attacks. Toward the end of their lives, I visited them at home and in the hospital. I was never good at saying goodbye. I wanted my family to live long lives. But they had to leave and I had to let them go. It was hard. My sorrow consumed me, the depths of my pain shown by shedding loud tears while I tried to understand why they had to die. I felt completely empty and emotionally drained after each death. It was difficult to listen to the comments of surviving relatives and friends who said, "At least, he didn't suffer long." But most of my relatives suffered whether it was a couple of months or years. In my dad's case, it was brutal and agonizing to watch his level of pain while trying to maintain his dignity, death like birth, is not easy. Often, I would hear people say during a wake, "Oh, he looks so real lying there in the casket." But there was nothing even remotely real to me when I looked inside that casket. The person was lifeless. Where was that person? Where did he really go?

Later, after I got married, my best friend, Karen committed suicide. She was in her early thirties when she died. I got the call from a friend when I was getting ready to go to an aerobics class. Karen and I were both young, we had so much to live for and do. Karen was incredibly beautiful and a gifted artist. I knew she was unhappy and going through some tough times. But I didn't recognize the tragic signs of despair and loneliness. I didn't see her deep pain. I wrestled with her death for a long time. Where did she go after killing herself?

I have been thinking a lot about death since my dad and mom died. I believe so strongly now that they are with me. They are communicating to me in unique ways. Let me give you an example. After my dad died, I went to his office in his home. I looked at his empty desk where he sat to pay our bills. I looked at the paneling he carefully and meticulously labored over in order to make this room masculine and a special man cave. He built bookcases, cabinets with drawers, furniture, and he even handcrafted the most beautiful bar in our family room—he was so immensely handy. I remember the nights after work, when he would spend hours building us this modern home in the suburbs. He was so proud of this home. So, in his office remembering, I sat on the floor in front of the cabinet drawers. Next to them were several low shelves housing unlabeled photo albums. I chose one album not knowing what pictures I might find inside those worn pages. The album I randomly chose slipped to the floor and opened right side up at my feet. And there in front of my eyes was a picture of dad with his arm around my shoulders. I was an adult in this picture and I remember when the picture was taken. When that photo album opened to that picture of us, I recall thinking *Dad wanted me to know he is OK and that he will always have his arms around me.* He was not really gone. I felt his presence.

There are other stories of mom and dad communicating with me since their deaths. I sense their existence in unusual circumstances. They seem to be more normal for me now. Their memories come in my dreams, in songs, in words.

One particular morning, upon awakening, I noticed that one large window pane had a big rectangular sheet of condensation—only on one window! It was peculiar to me that to the left of the window was the word "Hi." The word printed very legibly as if someone needed to say hello. At first, I thought I was hallucinating. I grabbed my glasses on the nightstand and took another look. The word was still there. Very visible! I asked my husband to look at the rectangle in the window. He saw the perfectly formed condensation. It reminded me of a sheet of paper affixed to the glass. I asked my husband if he saw anything else within or on the framed rectangle. He said he did not. I asked him to move closer to me; it was then that he too saw the word "Hi." I stared at the word. It did not disappear for a while. This word, I believe was a sign that my mom was near.

Later in the week, I went grocery shopping with my husband. We parked the car and entered the Big Y grocery market. Almost as soon as we entered, I heard the song *Fly Me to the Moon* by Frank Sinatra. This held such great significance for me because my dad sang all of Frank's tunes and he sounded just like him. He sang for the troops in the army during World War II, at home and in night clubs because he was so good. He would just pick up the microphone when asked to sing. I felt so reassured that day, that dad was telling me he was with mom and flying high.

There are so many other stories that I could share. But perhaps you are skeptical of my accounts. I don't blame you. All I can tell you is that I believe that death is not the end—that my family is still here and loving me, it makes me feel less alone. It makes me look at all creatures and the gifts of this earth as vital spiritual beings—stewards of this earth and all of its inhabitants.

I also know that my soul, my life energy will live on. I only hope that I can live today with grateful purpose, without fear –knowing that I am losing nothing in death but gaining in life.

Mini Morsel Sampling:

If this were your last day on earth, how would you spend it? Take a moment and write your own obituary. What would you like people to remember about you? If those memories do not align with where you are right now, what are you willing to do each day to become who you are in your obituary as compared to the person you are right now?

MINI MORSEL 7

Inferiority

I was always the shortest girl in my class both in elementary and high school. So, as a result, I was always selected to be in the front of the line, or in the front seat. I hated being singled out to lead the line. I wanted to experience the back of the line or the seat in the back of the room—at least once.

> "No one can make you feel inferior without your consent."
> ~ Eleanor Roosevelt

I was also the shyest student because my learning disabilities made reading, comprehension, and retention so difficult. The feelings of inferiority and insecurity were my closest companions. Some teachers who felt that they could accurately predict my miserable future of failure, contributed to the persistent realization that I was not as bright as my classmates were.

However, it soon became clear to me that I was not going to be a math wizard, nor was I going to be the smartest person in the world, but I was going to be a success in spite of my shortcomings (no pun intended). I was going to choose to discover my strengths, nurture a positive self-image, look at my problems rationally and find the best solution to solve them. I decided to maintain a hopeful outlook filled with gratitude, joy, and good self-care. I developed a greater sense of resiliency because I chose to learn and grow from difficult situations.

I know today that I would have not been an exceptional elementary and high school teacher had I not experienced the difficulties of learning. My creativity allowed me to reach out to youngsters who also lacked the writing, speaking, and critical thinking skills as I did. Together, we designed new ways of learning that was fun, innovative, and exciting. How thankful I am to have had the opportunity to struggle in school! I feel sorry for people who feel inferior and have not gotten over it. They attract and associate with those who feel the same pain, hating others and finding comfort in making them scapegoats. They will use any means to mask their feelings of inferiority and elicit the illusion of superiority.

Too bad they haven't realized that no one can make you feeling inferior without your consent!

> ***Mini Morsel Sampling:***
>
> *Remember a time when you felt left out or inferior for some reason. Now, step back and assess the circumstance surrounding your feelings. What can you do in the moment to become more resilient and hopeful about you? What trigger or cue can you use to remind you when you feel this way again, now that you have a different view point?*

It's easy to hold onto the mistakes we've made, and to think of ourselves as ugly or broken or guilty or confused. We have the voices in our heads that remind us of who we are not. We hear ourselves constantly being compared to others, thinking of ourselves as less than perfect. I think we should be thinking about our purpose in life. What are we being called to do? What is our intention? And how do we use the power of intention to find our purpose? I like to use affirmations to help me re-align my

"Those who love you are not fooled by mistakes you have made or the dark images you hold about yourself. They remember your beauty when you feel ugly, your wholeness when you are broken, your innocence when you feel guilty, and your purpose when you are confused."

values, re-visit my strengths and to reframe the negative voices and change them to positive affirmations.

I have made mistakes in my life but they do not trap me into feeling like I am a mistake or that I cannot use what I have learned from my mistakes, for the better. I have felt ugly in my life but I know deep down that I am not ugly; my beauty is within and that radiance shows through my smile. I have felt guilty and confused but I continue to ask for forgiveness and I have learned to forgive, the gift of forgiveness frees me.

So when I feel all those negative things, or hear the negative thoughts, and start to say negative words or phrases, I change them to positive affirmations. Instead of saying, "I am a mistake," I say "I am valuable." Instead of saying "I am not worthy," I say "I am worthy." Instead of saying "I am ugly," I say "I am beautiful as God intended me to be." Instead of saying "I am broken," I say "I am whole."

And I say these affirmations daily with gratitude for my life, remembering that I am loved unconditionally by family and friends.

> ***Mini Morsel Sampling:***
>
> *So what are your intentions? How will you use the power of intention to shape your new life? What do your affirmations look like? Write down one affirmation you can say aloud each day this week. Practice until that affirmation becomes your intention.*

Transition Time: Step Out of Your Comfort Zone

I remember this monologue from William Shakespeare's *As You Like It* as if I were on the stage in a theatre, reciting it. The poem always held meaning for me. Today, I realize that we are in transition—always evolving. If not, then we are in maintenance mode. We preserve or conserve our energy, our life purpose, move faster to the seventh age or death.

"All the world's a stage,
And all the men and women merely players.
They have their exits and their entrances,
And one man in his time plays many parts,
His acts being seven ages."

Transition or change is always difficult. I recognize that I get a bit scared when something new happens—when I have to step out of my comfort zone. However, when I really think about it, and change my perspective, stepping out can be an adventure or a challenge—a new experience with an unexpectedly pleasurable outcome. Moreover, if it is not the enjoyable experience I anticipated or expected, I face that encounter and know that I can take a new path. It is important in each stage of our life to embrace the moment savoring each occasion so we can grow.

A retiree contacted me recently to coach him in ways to find new opportunities for mental and social interactions. It occurred to me that he is resistant to change, "I am a lazy retiree," he said. He added that he wanted more motivation, meaning, and challenge in his life. However, when I asked him if he is ready to experiment, not knowing the outcome, but going for the experience, he said he already knew what to do. He didn't need me. As I further explored with him as to why he just doesn't do what he knows he needs to, his silence made it clear that he is comfortable with where he is currently. Why? Because he would have to step out of his comfort zone, become more sociable instead of watching television and dwelling on the terrible events of the day. He then shared that he was always shy and a loner. That statement suggested that he might have some difficulties in making new social contacts. However, his wife and son are concerned about him, worried that he is not mentally and socially stimulated. His negativity and resistance towards trying new things was so strong that there is no space for new explorations, thoughts, and creations to emerge. He is moving toward his seventh age instead of transitioning towards a fuller, more focused life.

It is my hope that you will take steps to move away from resistance, to embrace your open space, and let even the most uncomfortable experiences or memories bring you to more positive and purposeful life. In that space, you can continue to emerge into the person you were meant to be at any stage or age of your life.

Mini Morsel Sampling:

So, what is holding you back? Fear of success or failure? What life stage are you currently in? How can you move away from resistance and let your uncomfortableness be a time for awakening?

Tomorrow's Second Chance

I am so eternally grateful for the teachers, administrators, and recruiters who believed in me and gave me a second chance.

I am dyslexic; I didn't know this during elementary school. In grade school, when I couldn't read, write, or comprehend well, I used to think that I was stupid. Being told that I wouldn't amount to anything, telling me that I wouldn't be accepted to a college or even if I did, the university would be one that the sisters (at the private school) would select for me. Conveniently, the chosen college was run by the same order of sisters as my convent.

The nuns decided for me that the college I should attend was run by the Sisters of the Presentation of Mary in Nashua, New Hampshire; an all girls' college. In retrospect, I think the sisters were out to recruit me to pledge my life to their religious order. I wasn't even given the opportunity to select a major. I was haphazardly thrown into Liberal Arts curricula. I was most miserable with my situation at the school.

After my first year of college, this unhappy overweight young woman decided to search for a college that she wanted to attend. I wanted to study acting or something more creative. I wanted to study in a large city not somewhere in the outskirts of cold New Hampshire, where I had spent my freshman year. Granted my SAT scores from high school were poor. Nevertheless, I knew what I could do well in oral interpretation and acting.

I chose to go to Boston, Massachusetts and I chose Emerson College for oral interpretation and acting. My SATS were so low that the college refused me, but during my interview, I was asked to read from a script and demonstrate my talent. The admissions officer was impressed! I was granted entrance to Emerson on probation. The school gave me my second change to prove myself, and I did! I excelled in school because I loved what I was studying. I loved the excitement of the city. I was given a new tomorrow.

All through my life, I have asked that I not be judged by what is on paper but what I can accomplish. Results-driven, I was given opportunities because I didn't quit and certain people really believed in me.

I haven't forgotten the amazing individuals who gave me second chances. I hope you remember those who believed in you too. And it is my wish that you take this challenge to give someone's tomorrow a second chance. Who knows, they just might make an incredible difference in this world and maybe in your world.

Mini Morsel Sampling:

Everyone needs a second chance at something. What would your new tomorrow look like if you were given a second chance? What positive actions can you take to create the different day after?

Women! Rise Up!

- Women! Rise Up!
- Stand shoulder to shoulder
- Arms entwined, heads held high
- Hold tight the barricade of your bodies

- Fortify yourself
- Against the weight of the crowd
- As they push you, lunge at you
- To beat and drive you down
- They will try to suffocate you
- Condemn you without rightful cause
- And show no mercy.
- They will rape, pillage, and rob you of your dignity
- But they will not win
- Remain steadfast in your search
- To fight for truth and justice
- You too have human and civil rights
- Guaranteed under the law
- Even though rulings are often unequal
- Partial to the one-sided allegations
- Made against the women of the world
- You have a voice, you have a story.
- You have a right to be heard.
- No matter what atrocity against your being
- Is forced upon you; whatever you face
- Stay strong. Fight. Persist together.
- You have a voice.
- Your song will harmonize and fill the emptiness
- As one global melody resonating change
- Women! Rise Up!

Mini Morsel Sampling:

Irrespective of your gender or sexual orientation, you are entitled to a voice. How do you want to be heard? What steps are you willing to take? How can you make a difference in what you believe to be just and true?

Second Chance and Tomorrow's Challenge

Daylight Savings Time!

I am so grateful for this time change! I can enjoy the drive home from work at 6:30 p.m. because I can operate my vehicle with the intention to savor the sights and sounds that often go unnoticed, during our dark, winter night commutes.

As I deliberately and mindfully observed residences, signs, animals, and the potholes on my drive home last night, the first day of daylight savings, I delighted in seeing tiny buds popping out of the ground. The springtime gives us a new opportunity to seek pleasure in their rebirth after a long winter.

Tomorrow and each day going forward, we have the opportunity to share the earth's second chance of providing for our needs. Our challenge is our second chance at being responsible! We seem to expect earthly provisions without working for them, taking care of them; without appreciating their origin.

> ### *Mini Morsel Sampling:*
>
> *Most of us were nurtured growing up. We were sowed with seeds of good words, the love of neighbor, and respect for all people. Tomorrow's challenge is giving our world a second chance. Tomorrow is our second chance at restoration, reconciliation, and rebuilding. How many of you are up to the challenge of a second chance? And what will you do?*

MINI MORSEL 8

Compassion

The little organ that can... but can't destroy me or you! It is interesting that human beings have a little, organ in our mouths known as the tongue; that tongue can destroy or heal a person in an instant. It is our choice to decide how to use our tongue—to hurt or restore through our words.

> "Compassion is the keen awareness of the independency of all things."

How do we choose our words? We can be mindfully careful about how we select our words...carefully constructing them to uplift each other. We have the power and resources to rebuild lives, and that takes time and energy. It takes time to see things from another perspective and to walk in the shoes of another.

I am writing about this subject in order to plead with you to think about what you say this week. Why? Words are being said about me to destroy and hurt me. There is an unfair picture being painted about me and that is untrue. I have been cast out, eliminated, and erased from view. I know the pain of having rumors destroy my very being. However, I know that there is someone out there, who knows the truth about who I am. So I hold on to that thought. That comforts me. If you are feeling a similar pain, remember who you really are. Take solace. Hold on to your faith.

Mini Morsel Sampling:

Remember, the little organ that could, can't destroy me or you! Discuss or write down, how this little organ left you feeling destroyed in the past. Now that you have experienced that hurt, how you can prevent yourself from being engaged in gossiping, bullying, or hurting others with your words? What will you remember about the pain you felt? Don't let a bully's tongue sever current and future relationships.

In the silent stillness

- In the silent stillness, I heear wisdom speaking
- Awakening my sleepy inner self
- Coaxing me to explore, discover and pursue
- The authentic, magical, spiritual me

- My journey's path much traveled, led me
- To experiences unwanted at times, but so necessary for growth
- In the silent stillness, wisdom is urging me to face life
- With courage, determination, and resilience
- To take avenues untraveled with desire, vision, and persistence
- To choose confidence, erasing fear and nagging doubt
- My mental acuity is heightened, bringing me to
- The person I am meant to be now...the dreams today that I hold sacred...
- The hope for meaning as I listen to wisdom in the stillness of silence

Mini Morsel Sampling:

Acting and speaking with confidence or conviction on a passionate subject matter takes courage. But you are strong, resilient, and determined...so fight for the confidence. Do more research on the issue that you want to know more about, experience the growing pains as you prepare to act and speak; fighting with the conviction and passion that you have inside you.(1) So what are you acting upon?(2)What will you voice out with confidence? (3) Spend a few minutes in silence every day. Enjoy the peaceful solitude. What is your wisdom in the stillness of silence telling you? Keep a daily journal.

A HEART WIDE OPEN...FOR EACH OTHER

If I were undergoing open heart surgery, you would see my heart exposed. You would see the scars from the pain, joy from the happy memories, and the apparent defects that need repair or replacement.

You may say that my heart looks like most human beings anatomically speaking. However, if you look deep beyond the surface, you will observe the emotional blockages that cause my heart to skip its beats or pump blood too fast, leaving me breathless. Over time, continued chronic stress to the heart can trigger heart failure.

So, I try to control anxiety, pain, and fear with exercise, organic food, and some medicines. All these preventive measures certainly are worth doing.

I distance myself from the trigger to cope with the emotional anguish. I compartmentalize my emotions. Then, I do not feel so overwhelmed. Perhaps it is not the best way to deal with confrontation, but I need time to evaluate, analyze, and revisit my heart to see what it is telling me. I need to be still and listen to my heart's voice.

So, when life just seems too difficult and I cannot handle one more thing on my plate, I choose to bypass my *blocked arteries* as a means to heal, and I distance myself from everyone. I realize I need a time out to focus on me. My heart is wide open for everyone. I will always be the person that loves and cares for people unconditionally. Maybe that is why my heart, hurts, grieves, and mourns for those who believe that their hearts are more righteous, more honest and more deserving than the next person.

My heart carries my blood to various parts of my body without my asking, just like yours. One thing I know for certain is that it will stop beating one day.

For now, I will continue to keep my heart wide open to give and receive love in the only way I know.

Mini Morsel Sampling:

How can we keep our hearts wide open for each other?

How open is your heart today? How vulnerable are you willing to be?

Triggering behavior change: You don't have to pull the trigger!

It always amazes me how genuine we are when we want to change an unhealthy behavior but when push comes to shove, we just don't. We get sidetracked and that makes our vision for a healthier life, pretty impossible.

As a teacher, I looked for ways to help children change improper behavioral responses in academic or social confrontations. I proactively allowed students to use critical thinking skills to find more appropriate methods of behavior to resolve conflict. After all, I reasoned, they will eventually join the workforce and find jobs that require critical thinking skills grounded in fair mindedness, effective communication competencies peppered with exceptional listening skills and thoughtful, positive engagement by bringing enthusiasm and passion to their work environment.

As a former entrepreneur of a fitness business and currently, a positive performance life coach who guides individuals to find simple means to take action to reach their goals; I see that there is a formula to get to the finish line. It is Fogg's behavior model: B=mat (Behavior equals motivation, ability and triggers).

Three things must occur simultaneously in order for change to happen. There must be motivation, the task (what the person chooses to do) must be easy—so that there is immediate success (a reward), and there must be a trigger to remind the individual to initiate the new behavior.

We know that behavior is a learned habit repeated over time so that it becomes an automatic response to an action, thought, or emotion. To break a habit takes time and old behavior patterns need to be replaced by new, healthier, and productive patterns. Easier said than done? Yes. But it is not impossible.

Motivation can be high but if the ability to do something is too hard for the person, the habit or behavior does not change long term. If the goal is long-lasting behavior, then the motivation has to match what the person wants to do, In other words, understand what you want to do and then find the resources to do what you already want to do. The focus should be on the behaviors you want that is easy to do (small steps) with a trigger acting as a prompt or reminder.

Let's take exercise, for example. Clients tell me that they want to add a fitness program to their day. But they choose the *all or nothing* approach. They sometimes decide on unrealistic goals that set them up for immediate failure like "I will exercise for forty five minutes each day!" When they haven't exercised for that period of time each day as avowed, they become disenchanted and give up. Another example might be a client who wants to reduce the amount of soda that they consume in a day. So the unrealistic goal might be to remove all soft drinks from the house. But the more realistic approach might be to reduce the amount of six sodas a day to three in the first week or two.

Clients often come to me highly motivated to change but find that they cannot succeed because the tasks they created for themselves are much too great. Plus, they omit the last component of this behavior change model— a trigger design! Designing a trigger such as a piece of string around a finger or an alarm that rings to remind you to act now needs implementation on a daily basis.

Let's take the first client who decides on a daily forty-five minute walking program. He comes home after work, checks his mail, phone messages, and emails and then finds that the time for walking has come and gone. A trigger for him might be leaving his sneakers and warm up clothes by the door to remind him that his first priority upon arriving home is the walk. And, instead of starting with forty-five minutes, he could change it to twenty minutes twice that week (an easier activity and one he can accomplish). He chooses to mark his weekly calendar with the days and times for those walks (another trigger, the calendar), checking off the days he successfully completed his exercise commitment. He might be saying upon arriving home that he didn't feel like walking after a hard day, but his verbal recognition of *I did it* gives him the impetus to challenge himself for the next walk, increasing the pace and the time by five minutes.

The second client can use a trigger at work to drink a cup of water instead of soda. The trigger can be his cell phone vibrating each ninety minutes to remind him to get up and go to the water cooler for a sip of water. And he can monitor the amount of soda at home by only putting three sodas instead of six in the fridge for the next two weeks, monitoring the amount to decrease his soft drink intake over time. The task for this client is doable. He has the motivation that matches what he can commit to. He chose the easy-to-do ability, and he found triggers that help to remind him of his commitment. Eventually, the behavior changes for the better.

As a positive performance coach, I firmly believe in celebrating with clients, their accomplishments. Each little new learned behavior helps build the ultimate outcome—their vision of a more healthy life. Sending positive affirmations and pointing out to the small accomplishments made, builds positive reinforcement.

Mini Morsel Sampling:

*I challenge you to look at the behaviors you wish to change, find motivation, and an activity as well as a trigger to help you change the behavior. If you need guidance in motivation assessment, trigger choosing, goal setting and negative self-talk, contact me. Let's get you to where you want to be without pulling a trigger; and instead, finding the most effective **triggers** that work for you. What performance do you want to change? Write down 3 triggers that will help you today with a better behavior choice.*

Walls or Bridges?

How high do we build walls and how deep do we cement the footings of a structure to keep people from climbing over or tunneling under them? I believe that there is no wall too tall or too cavernous to keep people out.

I also believe that in creating walls to keep the outsiders away, we are really building walls around our hearts. We keep people out symbolically as we disconnect with them, when we do not see others as valuable contributors to our world.

Our diversities make us better equipped to bring our knowledge and expertise to the table to design new solutions to our global problems.

We need bridges designed to reach across regions of the world that need our help; and support us in return. We need bridges of love, compassion, and empathy that foster dreams in each of us.

Our fortification against crime, illegal drugs, and other illegal activities does not give us answers. They contribute to the endless trivial squabbles that divide us; cutting us off, leaving us isolated and detached.

I wonder if we will ever stop building walls and instead erect bridges with open hearts and minds; as the center for discovery and invention. I wonder if it is possible for humans to put aside the barricade and embrace each other. Empower each other to find remedies for those things that can destroy us.

__Mini Morsel Sampling:__

What do you think? Walls or bridges? Research "walls" built to divide societies. What has happened? What can you learn from history? What do you know about bridges? How can you use a bridge as a symbol to unite instead of divide?

Be the Tallest Poppy

This morning I was weeding the garden; not a task that I was relishing. You see, the heavy rains had produced the most stubborn weeds I have ever had to pull. Nevertheless, I persevered determined to complete at least one section near the lower patio.

While weeding, I started thinking about a line that I read recently—b*e the tallest poppy*. I don't have any poppies in my garden, but I had the tallest weeds ever! Contrasting to that, I had the smallest, weeds whose roots seemed to extend miles below the earth's surface. They were the most difficult one's to unearth. They clung ever downward like someone keeping their nose to the ground and out of trouble. Yet, what trouble they caused! Those weeds whose roots extended below also reached out to the side like long tentacles wrapping themselves around other plants and flowers, suffocating them.

And, the tall weeds whose roots I would have guessed more difficult to extract were uprooted with one gentle pull. Interesting.

I like the idea of being the tallest poppy. I think for me it means being visible, a leader–who is recognized for my accomplishments or achievements. I like the idea of standing out for what I believe in but being flexible enough to move and be transplanted in another garden. And there, I imagine I would enjoy finding new relationships, learning new skills, growing taller, and becoming even more of a wiser and compassionate leader. I don't like keeping my nose to the ground because then I wouldn't notice what is going on around me, I wouldn't be making changes or challenging others to change.

On another note others might be jealous of the tallest Poppy. So, they may want to cut it down because they want the distinction, the recognition or the praise for themselves. They fear that the leader will be controlling and become aggressive. So, like the small weeds, they attack quietly but viciously until the tallest poppy is cut down to size. But I would rather be cut down than stay low to the ground, unnoticed and not changing myself or the system around me.

Mini Morsel Sampling:

Former Prime Minister Margaret Thatcher said "Let your poppies grow tall." How tall are yours? And how will you use your leadership abilities (your Tallest Poppy) to make the world a better place?

Beauty or Beast

There is a beautiful person inside each of us, but there is also a beast. It is our choice which one to feed each day.

We can notice the beauty physically around us, the loveliness in each other (in the exquisite soul of an individual). We can take delight in the moment we meet another person, maybe even someone who appears quite different from us physically. And in our differences, we may see a familiar face—ourselves. Greet the mirror image of ourselves and breathe compassion in the world with just one act of kindness showered on a person we don't know. A simple gesture is all that is needed. A sense of real caring about people unlike us but who share our human race.

Or we can focus on the beast that we all carry inside of us—the one that feeds hatred, greed, vengeance, blame, and self-righteousness. We can let the events of the day from the news, our home, our job, and on the road feed our anger leading us down the path of savage behavior.

We can fuel our own feelings of entitlement, power, and control to join others in becoming beast like. We can continue abusing, killing, acting unjustly only to send a message that this is what we are meant to be. We can continue in this same pattern and the legacy we leave to our children and the community will imitate our behavior.

Or we can take measured steps to remind ourselves each day of how similar we all are in our differences. We all hold the same hopes and dreams. We all want the important things: love, trust, friendship and peace. However, we cannot even envision a peaceful world or a community until we address and confront the inner beast inside us each and every day.

Mini Morsel Sampling:

What are you called to be today? Who are you feeding— the beauty inside you or the beast? It is always your choice.

R.E.C. Do you have it?

Each New Year, I wonder what the year will have in store for us. Will we see more suffering and inhumanity towards our fellow men as in past years? Will we continue to witness innocent children gunned down by individuals who show little caring for others? Will we read more accounts of cyber-bullying that devastates families and friends as they learn that their children and neighbor's children abruptly ended their lives as a result of the cruel treatment and endless teasing?

There are movements and organizations striving to end our indifference. And this is good.

But what I propose is that we embrace R.E.C. and communicate the message, then skillfully teach and share how to R.E.C.

What is R.E.C.? This acronym stands for Respect, Empathy, and Compassion.

I really feel like we have lost respect for each other. We rarely recognize or appreciate one another. Respectful language and behavior is not highly regarded in our world. Some people earn the respect of individuals by assisting others or playing important social roles. In many cultures, individuals are considered to be worthy of respect until they have proved otherwise. Courtesies that show respect include simple words and phrases like *thank you*, simple physical gestures like a slight bow, a smile or direct eye contact. When I was a child, it was a common courtesy to stand when an adult entered a room, when it was polite to share a firm handshake. I remember when we felt proud to stand in class or at a game to recite the pledge of allegiance and to bow our heads in silence. I remember when it was discourteous to talk back to a teacher and how our parents rebuked us for our rude behavior.

How can we teach respect? We teach our children to respect themselves, their skills and talents, their voice, their performance and style. Then we can instruct them to respect the talents, style, space, instruments, voice and performance of others, without envy but with amity. And we can teach our children to respect the property of all—their belongings—a chair, stereo, toys, and books. Respect is earned; we earn it by learning how to be respectful. Here are some helpful reminders that will help teach respect:

I am respectful of other people because that is the way I want to be treated. I am considerate of other people. I treat people with civility, courtesy, and dignity. I accept personal differences. I work to solve problems without violence. I never intentionally ridicule, embarrass, or hurt others.

The letter E in R.E.C. stands for empathy. Empathy means understanding another's feelings—the ability to identify with and understand somebody else's feelings or difficulties. Empathy is seeing with the eyes of the other, listening with the ears of another, and feeling with the heart of another, without judgment. It is just like thinking what if that were me? Putting yourself in the shoes of another can give us a new perspective of what that person may be seeing, hearing, or feeling.

And the last letter in R.E.C. is C which stands for compassion. We need to teach our children self-compassion for if we do not love ourselves, we cannot love or show compassion to others. When I think of compassion, I think of compassion in action. "When I was hungry, you gave me food; when I was thirsty, you gave me drink; I was a stranger and you took me in; I was naked and you clothed me; I was sick and you visited me; I was in prison and you came to me." Our children need to be taught through community service acts of compassion.

As the Dalai Lama said: "Love and compassion are necessities not luxuries. Without them, humanity cannot survive."

Mini Morsel Sampling:

I challenge you to practice and teach R.E.C. every day whether you are a child, teen or adult. Help humanity survive and thrive!

MINI MORSEL 9

Fear

What do athletes think about as they compete? Do they ever feel fear or nervous before their game? Ian Thorpe collected two Olympic title golds in the 400 meters freestyle. Inge DeBruijn, a female swimmer won three individual goals, and Lenny Krayzelburg completed the 100/299 double at the 2000 Sydney Olympics. I bet you think that these amazing athletes who train hard, overcame injuries never experience nervousness

"Nothing in life is to be feared, it is only to be understood. Now is the time to understand more, so that we may fear less." Marie Curie

"People ask me... what was going through your mind in the race? And I don't know. I try and ...let my body do what it knows."
Ian Thorpe,
Swimming
Champion

before a race. Well, maybe they feel some nervousness but not the kind that you and I might feel if we were swimming in the Olympics. They are experienced swimmers, after all! Nevertheless, let me tell you that their inner belief is challenged just like ours. What do they do to overcome their fears?

One thing is for sure—you cannot get rid of nervousness. Neither can the athlete. It will be there like stage fright. But you can use the fear and work through it. Nervousness is energy and when used to your advantage, you can perform well in spite of the doubts that you may have. You can even win the race!

Athletes use this nervous energy to their advantage. It is interesting to know that if a swimmer, an athlete, or any kind of performer is not nervous at all before an event, they may not have the power or the energy required to perform their best or win. Athletes train their mind and body to deal with self-doubt.

As Craig Townsend said in his article *Nervousness is Energy-Sports Psychology Tips for Swimmers*, "being a little nervous is an advantage, not a disadvantage. This is what nervousness is for – to give you energy. Remember this in your next big race – channel the nerves into your swim, and feel your body unleash the incredible power it has been storing up for the race. Your mind will always provide what your body needs – and one of these things is nervous energy."

To all potential winners, let your body do what it knows best, but make sure you use your nervous energy to your advantage!

Mini Morsel Sampling:

We all want to perform better as an executive, student, athlete, teacher, or an actor...whatever our calling is. However, it takes practice, both physically and mentally. Our nervousness often controls how our body and mind reacts to a situation, event or sport. However, if we can block distractions such as the jitters, we can control the critical voice that feeds our mind. Techniques such as visualization, meditation, and self-talk exercises help break the apprehension cycle and improve performance. Try visualizing yourself winning (at work, play, and home); feel your body as it relaxes into the routine; hear the sounds become silent as you focus on your task. What can you say to yourself when your nerves appear? Positive self-talk needs as much practice as any activity. What can you say to yourself when you start doubting yourself and the negative talk begins to surface? Try closing your eyes, breathing diaphragmatically, and quietly begin a short mediation. Let your body relax and draw in pictures in your mind of a positive outcome. See it and believe.

I like this quote. Why? Because I think, we hold onto fears and that limits our potential. I know personally that I have wrestled with fears. I know that it can paralyze and halt progress. However, I can choose to fear my ability, my self-worth, or even the people I don't know. I

> "Nothing in life is to be feared, it is only to be understood. Now is the time to understand more, so that we may fear less."
> Marie Curie

can choose to fear the things at which I might fail and never have the joy of trying something new and risky.

However, if I choose to experiment and test those things that I fear, I may find the results to be rewarding and surprisingly exciting. I may even find a cure. And, if I do fail (there is the chance of failure), the experiment will lead me to a new understanding...perhaps a greater one. I just need to remember there is nothing to fear. Fear will hold me back. It will prevent me from becoming the person I am meant to be.

My message to you this week is **be curious**. Put an expiration date to your fears. Experiment wisely. Learn from your results.

Mini Morsel Sampling:

I will choose to be curious this week. I have experimented with being inquisitive and have learned this about myself____________.

Do you remember the Cowardly Lion in the Wizard of Oz who in spite of his fear exhibited great courage?

He was the king of beasts, and as such, he was expected to be courageous—fearless

> "You gain strength, courage and confidence through every experience in which you really stop to look fear in the face...you must do the thing you think you cannot do." Eleanor Roosevelt

and powerful. But this king of beasts lacked bravery. He told Dorothy that he was very fearful and that he wanted to find courage. So, he teamed up with Dorothy who wanted to go home to Kansas, Scarecrow who wanted a brain, and Tin Man who wanted a heart. Together they journeyed to Emerald City where they believed the great Oz would give them their wishes. Only this adventure proved to be a journey of self-discovery for each of the characters.

For as the cowardly lion continued on his travel to the magical Emerald City to get his badge of courage, he reacted to scary situations with tremendous bravery often without thinking or deliberating about what to do. He just did!

It is interesting to me that I often hear clients say that they are afraid, even when it comes to losing weight. They have failed too many times to attempt to try again.

Their fear is so ingrained in their psyche that they stay fearful, shameful, and reluctant to face the fear of failure that holds them from achieving their dream.

Doing what you are terrified of, despite the fear of past mistakes or failures, teaches us courage, strength, and resilience.

Let me suggest that you act in the face of fear with excitement and anticipation for something wonderful to happen. Don't wait for some kind of *magic or power* to change you and your thoughts. There is courage and strength within each of us—we just have to find it—just like the cowardly lion. He had the strength and courage within him—no magical wizard could give him that valor.

You too, have the courage and strength to do what you need to do, whatever you need to do. There is no magic in that, the magic lies within **you**! So, wave your magic wand and enjoy the process.

Mini Morsel Sampling:

I am finding courage within me in this moment by_________________. I will practice being gutsy by changing my thoughts from _______________________ to _____________________.

MINI MORSEL 10

Money/Greed/Vengeance

The Unforgiving Heart
His heart beats furiously
inside its chambers
Pounding like giant waves
against its arteries
Pressure silently, secretively
building
Inviting clots to mingle in its
chambers
Pumping angry blood backwards
Creating massive muscle trauma
Valves emitting signals of
Distress, suffering and pain
Its outer structures' detaching
Logical feelings and emotions
Forming impenetrable outer crusts
Cement-like, hardened to the core

"We make a living by what we get but we make a life by what we give." Winston Churchill

So vindictive
So callused by hearsay
It kills
Not the accused but the accuser.

Mini Morsel Sampling:

What do you do with your anger? What can you do to temper your anger? How can you choose your initial anger reaction to something more calming and appeasing?

Venomous Viper & Poisonous Minds

- The viper slithers in the rainforest's darkness
- Unnoticed, hidden, veiled from its victim
- Its binocular-like eyes darting in clandestine rhythm
- Secreting venomous, implicating defamations
- Slipping quietly among the tall weeds
- His fangs hiss in merciless taunts
- In condemnation, accusation, fabrications
- Believable to the evil snake and his cohorts
- As he and his followers prepare to accurately emit poison
- Striking and envenoming its prey carefully planned and rehearsed
- Then releasing it to the elements, ever watchful
- Until it strikes again gainfully following

- The injured defenseless creature
- Until the viper's predator stops and dies
- And the hunted creature is swallowed up.
- For now, the poisoned minds who incited the viper
- Appears triumphant; albeit the verdict not yet revealed
- The Judgment - the victorious is the victim.

Wishing...

- My wish for you and the world is
- Less conflict and more conversation
- Less vacillation and more resolution
- Less jealousy and more good will
- Less unfairness and more justice
- Less hard-heartedness and more compassion
- Less hatred and more unconditional love for all living breathing creatures
- Less loneliness and more companionship
- Less blame and more forgiveness
- Fewer takers and more givers
- And lastly, my wish for you is less adversity and more blessings

Mini Morsel Sampling:

This is my wish. What's yours?

MINI MORSEL 11

Balance and Serenity

Question: Why is it that we rush from one thing to the next? Why are we always in a hurry? Yet, we yearn for balance, and simplicity. Remember when life was simple? When life was easier, simple and less hectic! Remember...

- When people had time to talk to you not text you!
- When the community mattered!

"Serenity is not freedom from the storm but peace amid the storm."

Balance activity with serenity...

"Balance activity with serenity, wealth with simplicity, persistence with innovation, community with solitude, familiarity with adventure, constancy with change, leading with following." Jonathan Lockwood Huie

- When people smiled more!
- When people were alone but not lonely.
- When people enjoyed a bit of adventure but still sought quiet time to reflect and ponder.
- When people knew when to lead and when to follow and not feel threatened by either.
- When people seemed constant. There for you when you needed them, but also changing and growing for the better.
- When people felt wealthy in the things that matter (the simple, basic things) in life.

Mini Morsel Sampling:

Balance is essential. How are you balancing your life so that you don't miss out on the things that REALLY matter?

MINI MORSEL 12

Possibilities and Opportunities

The Train, the Cap, and the Gift

Picture this. You are on a crowded commuter train. It is the rush hour and you are tired. A young man enters your train compartment. He appears to be dressed like a rapper. Tattooed, wearing dark glasses with a gold chain around his neck. His cap is askew on his head. He holds a large boom box on one shoulder, and then places it on the floor. He turns and loudly announces "I want to stay out of trouble tonight." Heads bob up from their business to view this person. It is a quick look; passengers ignore him. Maybe he will disappear. Then, he blasts his music disturbing the quiet hum of the train's wheels on the track. Angry eyes look towards the boom box; the

> "Let your imagination release your imprisoned possibilities."

passengers' faces contort to reveal great displeasure at this disturbance. Then, the young man performs handstands, twirls in rhythm to the music, magically moving across the aisle that fascinates even the most annoyed passenger. All eyes are now focused on this talented person, his clothing and demeanor no longer seemingly a threat. At the end of his performance, the young man bows and, taking his cap off his head, offers it to the passengers. One by one, the passengers place money in the cap as they enthusiastically applaud.

Now, the doors of the train car open and some passengers depart. A homeless man enters the car. He smells. He finds a seat. All the occupants look down and they avoid looking at him. But they know he is there. Maybe if they ignore him, he will disappear. But he stays; and, as the train begins to move, he takes his hat off his head and entreats the occupants to place money in his hat. No one does. He finds a seat, gathering his plastic bags tightly around him. It is at that moment that the young rapper walks to the homeless man and pours his money from his cap into the homeless man's hat.

I coach people to see life as an opportunity. We have so many chances to change or touch lives.

Think about this. Your life is like the train traveling to different destinations. Each stop along your way, you can decide what you will do to make an impact or a difference. You can choose to ignore, to stereotype or classify people and avoid them. Alternatively, you can choose to notice, appreciate differences, and to give back. Generosity doesn't take much—a smile, a kind word or a cup of coffee. Whatever you choose to do, I know your train stops will be much more fascinating. And you may find your life becoming more enthralling.

Turning Impossible to Possible!

Have You Ever Wondered…?

Why some people stay stuck in the same joyless job, relationship, or environment for years dreaming about a change, but not moving forward?

Why can others move past immense obstacles, find success, fulfillment, and leave a legacy?

I have witnessed clients, colleagues, and family members virtually stay imprisoned in a life without purpose or meaning. I have watched them contemplate change but not take the necessary giant step forward. Why?

Two words they often say: "I can't!" This really means "I won't!"

It's interesting to listen to people dance around why they can't do something, why they can't change, or why they can't be healthier. There are so many phenomenal excuses. I can write the book of excuses because I have heard them all. I know from experience that we often sabotage ourselves by creating protective walls that keep us comfortable. Sometimes the walls become so thick that it seems impossible to break free from the safety of our comfort zone. It seems impossible to find new ways to overcome obstacles.

Moving Past the Obstacles

One evening on my radio show "What's Weighing You Down?" I interviewed Leo, a man who was born and raised in Romania under the Communist rule. Leo shared his amazing journey of self-discovery, determination, and ambition to turn the impossible to possible. Leo told his story of living in a country where you did not have the choice to live your dream. You were told what to think, how to act, and what to do for a living. Leo explained that he and his family woke up at 4 a.m. on Saturday mornings so that all his five family members could shower before the hot water was shut off. Living in Romania under Communism meant going to bed at 10 p.m. because all the electricity throughout the city was shut off, even the streetlights. Obtaining groceries required a well-planned strategy. According to Leo, every family member had an assignment. Leo would go to the bread line. Cristi, his brother, to the butter line. Daniela, his sister, to the milk line, and his parents to the chicken line. And the chicken line meant chicken feet, necks and heads. There was no such thing as a chicken breast. Leo described his life as fearful. He and his family were afraid to talk about a better life or how to change their situation because they were scared that someone would hear, arrest, and detain them. You couldn't trust anyone not even your best friend! Leo clarified that the people of Romania were brainwashed to believe that their way of life was the only way. There was nothing more.

But Leo wanted more. By six years old, Leo, frustrated with his life, started lashing out. This oppressive environment was so harsh that the only way Leo could release his unhappiness was through fighting. One of his neighbors saw Leo's deep discontent and brought him to a wrestling room which proved to be Leo's ticket to life. This metaphorical meaning of fighting for his life proved to Leo that he was strong, stronger than the Communist mentality. Leo wanted to stand out, to be the best, and be different. He wanted an identity and felt that through wrestling, he could be the best. This was his opportunity.

Planning for the Future

Leo now knew something. He wanted to be free. He dared to dream big–to escape Romania! But to escape, he needed a career. Over the years, Leo became passionate about wrestling. He was 14 when he competed in his first World Championship and placed 4th in Istanbul, Turkey. Leo realized that being an athlete was the best ticket to freedom. Wrestling was very hard on Leo. He had to lose a lot of weight, undergo long hours of training and suffering. He explained that he spent many years starving in order to make his weight class for different competitions. Sometimes, he went without eating and drinking for days at a time. He and the other athletes were under constant pressure, and they were threatened to be sent home if they didn't do well. Finally, in 1999, Leo's wrestling team had scheduled a trip to the United States Olympic training center to train with the U.S. Olympic Wrestling team. Last minute, the trip was cancelled. Leo also told me that his passport was being held by the Romanian Wrestling officials. Another obstacle stood in Leo's way of realizing his dream. Nevertheless, Leo was determined to change his life and resigned his job as a wrestler in the Romanian Army wrestling team. The military police went after Leo, harassed his family, and called him a deserter. Leo obtained his passport six months later, sold some wrestling equipment, borrowed $300 from a close friend, and bought a plane ticket to Los Angeles, CA. On November 3, 1999, he arrived in LA with $10 in his pocket, a backpack, and knowing only four words of English.

Finding Success, Fulfillment, and Leaving a Legacy

So what makes Leo different? After landing in LA, Leo went straight to work. He got a job as a dishwasher and janitor. He was very excited! He was a World Champion and Olympic aspirant working as a happy toilet cleaner and dishwasher. He never felt he was too good to do the menial work. He knew it was going to be a hard journey paved with different unfulfilling jobs and situations. But Leo was determined and willing to do whatever it took to reach his goal. He became the best dish/toilet washer in Hollywood. Next, Leo became a waiter while learning English. Then he learned how to drive a car. His next goal was to become a citizen. During his journey, he always asked himself if he was satisfied with what he was doing. He was happy with each job that was leading him to his big dream. Leo continued to wrestle and in only a few years, he won several California State Championships, trained several US Olympians and was invited to the United States Olympic Center in Colorado Springs to train the US wrestling team. Leo also started college but while attending, he was injured during the training. This was another obstacle but not a deal breaker. Leo could have tossed in the towel, complained, or whined saying "Why me?" But Leo's attitude was "How fast can I get back on track?"

Success=RESULTS

Getting back on track and staying focused helped Leo become a success. He saw results with every job and in every situation. He used his obstacles and turned them into opportunities which turned into possibilities. His attitude, coupled with keeping his eye on the goal and re-evaluating each opportunity, helped him become who he was meant to be. He dreamed big and was determined and willing to do menial jobs until his dream was fulfilled. During one of his wrestling seminars, he met Kelly who owned a private gym in Encino. Kelly introduced Leo to personal training. Leo was offered a job as a personal trainer there. Starting with one client a week, Leo set his goals and worked hard. Within a short time, he had 30 clients per week. His ultimate goal was to own his own personal training facility. Leo went from a toilet cleaner to a landscaper, to waiting tables, to owning his RESULTS, his own gym in around three years! He didn't take his paycheck and buy fancy cars but instead stayed focused–his eye was on the goal. He was passion-driven, seeking a better life. He didn't let anything stop him–obstacles, fears, limiting beliefs, nor what others thought. He remained positively optimistic. Leo's mantra is: it takes work, real work and commitment—but anything is possible!

Mini Morsel Sampling:

What is possible for you even if it seems impossible now?

21.4 million People will be diagnosed with cancer every year by 2030. Forty-one percent of all adults will develop cancer. That means out of 5 of your friends, 2 will be diagnosed. Some others maybe misdiagnosed. These are alarming statistics.

When my dad was diagnosed with colon and pancreatic cancer, he never thought that this was his life sentence. At my dad's age and given the cancer's advanced stage, he had a few treatment options. He did have colon surgery, but pancreatic surgery and treatment was not an option. Instead, Dad chose to live. He created possible ways to enjoy his moments surrounded by his family and friends. The doctors gave dad approximately six months to live. He lived for two years! Why or how did he defy the odds and outlive the doctor's prediction?

The book *The Biology of Belief* is groundbreaking in the field of New Biology. Author Dr. Bruce Lipton is a former medical school professor and a research scientist. His experiments, and that of other leading edge scientists, have examined in great detail the processes by which cells receive information. The implications of this research radically changed our understanding of life. It shows that genes and DNA do not control our biology; that DNA is controlled by signals from outside the cell, including the energetic messages emanating from our positive and negative thoughts. We have the power to change our minds.

> "I have learned to use the word impossible with the greatest caution."
> ~Wernher von Braun

It is interesting to me that my dad changed his mind to live as fully as possible until he felt like it was time for him to leave us. There have been other examples or stories of people who show the will to fight and live. While their bodies are ravaged, their minds direct healing energy to their cells until they decide to move on. We can choose life or death each day as we decide what is possible or impossible. We know that cancer cells live in all of us; that cancer can be brought on by stress and the body's immune system breaking down.

> ***Mini Morsel Sampling:***
>
> *What is possible for you to do today to reduce stress? What are you willing to do? Use the word impossible with caution: Impossible is nothing; possible is everything!*

I have always found it very interesting that when one door closes, another one opens, that is, if I am clearly seeing the open door. There have been times in my life when the door is wide open but I am too caught up in what I have lost (the closed door) to see the new opportunity. Regretting what might have been I stayed in a place of missed possibility.

"When one door closes, another door opens; but we so often look so long and so regretfully upon the closed door, that we do not see the ones which open for us."

But when I changed my perspective on closed doors–and looked with eyes wide open at the world, new and better doors magically appeared. These doors revealed places greater than I had ever dreamed or imagined. How foolish I was to remain in regret. How much more wiser I am now to remember to seek those open doors when others close!

I'm OK...I'm not OK...I'm broken...But I will be OK!

How many times have you asked someone, "How are you?"

And how many times have you heard the response, "I'm great! I'm wonderful! I'm peachy! I'm OK!"

And how many times have you answered that same question with a similar retort?

However, you know in your heart that the person you asked that question to, was not OK; and you are not OK. Instead, you both feel broken; distraught that things and situations are just not going your/their way.

What can you do when you know someone is really hurting or when you are really aching on the inside?

We cannot fix a person's sorrow but there are some things that we can do to make a difference. We can listen if that person shares their feeling of desperation, we can hold their hand or give them a hug, or we can pray for them. We can share stories of inspiration and healing. We can recommend therapists, ministers, rabbis or coaches whose compassionate experience and wisdom can be restorative. We can do the same for ourselves. We often say "I'm OK" when asked "How are you?," we are not OK, but the most important thing to remember is that we will all be OK, if we allow ourselves time to heal.

> ***Mini Morsel Sampling:***
>
> *What story can you share today either aloud or on paper to inspire others and heal yourself? How can that narrative benefit you and the people around you?*

Ten ways to be OK again

1. Acknowledge your pain or distress. Know when you are not OK and express it.
2. Seek help if you become too distraught, feel unable to cope or feel overwhelmed.
3. Talk to a trusted friend.

4. Walk outdoors. Getting fresh air and exercise helps support circadian rhythms and elevates serotonin levels.

5. Mediate. Setting aside a few minutes each day to sit quietly and free the mind from distractions has been proven to relax to the body, mind, and soul.

6. Write. Keep a journal and record your feelings without worrying about grammar or punctuation. Write for 10 minutes a day without putting your pen down. Let out your true feelings and thoughts. Be angry. Be sad. Be vulnerable. Be silly.

7. Pray and listen to what your inner voice is telling you about this experience. Learn from your challenge. Give back to others what you have acquired, as a result of your soul-searching.

8. In all things (good and bad), be grateful because one day, you will be OK. Just know that there will always be moments in your life when things are not going to go the way you hoped or planned. There will be a new direction that emerges, perhaps another path with a greater opportunity to make changes in your life or in the world in which you live.

9. Seek out professional help, if you need it. You are not weak; you are learning how to become stronger. Ministers, rabbis, doctors, therapists and coaches are trained to help you find the

answers that lie within you. No one but you has the answers to your trials. Professionals assist you in seeing what is best for you.

10. Show compassion not only to others but to yourself. Give yourself the permission to say "no," to sit and do nothing, to watch movies on your day off or read a book. And, most importantly, bring joy to other people in your daily walk. When you bring happiness to another human being, you temporarily forget your troubles; and as a result, your spirit will be lifted too.

Mini Morsel Sampling:

Pick two ways for you to be OK again. Write them down and practice doing them.

Continually Evolving

Who are you and who are you becoming?

This is not a trick question. It is a question that I ask myself on a regular basis. I guess you might say I am a work in progress. I am not done with life or becoming who I am meant to be. I am in the process, of being in the moment; yet, moving towards bringing my skills and talents to new heights. Sounds lofty, doesn't it? Seriously, I am not boasting. I truly believe we grow, if we allow ourselves to seek new possibilities, to venture into new territories; otherwise, I believe that we become stagnant. If we are quite active and full of energy; new excitement emerges, and we are open to experiences that may never have come our way if we had not been receptive.

> "The whole point of being alive is to evolve into the complete person you were intended to be."
> Oprah

My personal and professional background has been marred by some tragic but also joyous moments. I used to wonder why certain things happened; but now I know why they did. And, I am happy that they were a part of my life because today I am richer for it. I feel that all the experiences I have lived, all the job opportunities served me in a way that makes me who I am becoming.

I know with certainty that this new phase of my becoming is as exciting as my first career choice. I also know that it took time for me to discover who I am and who I am becoming. And, I recognize that I like helping people realize who they are becoming. Yes, it can be scary, but anything worth doing or accomplishing is a bit frightening. I know how to conquer that fear. I have taken that journey down the road to self-discovery and uncovered my life's purpose.

Mini Morsel Sampling:

Where has your life journey taken you so far? Connect the dots between where you started to where you are now. At each new juncture in your life, write down where you were headed and what purpose brought you to that place. See your future you. What are you doing? Who have you become? See yourself as if you are already there.

Who are you really? Are you a mother, father, spouse, lover, teacher, inventor, entrepreneur, artist, scientist?

That's what you do, not who you are. Who you are goes deeper than your outward appearance or your profession. You are an emotional, spiritual being capable of happiness or well-being. But isn't it interesting, that many of us are in love with suffering? That we choose pain instead of focusing on the habits of happiness!

> "Look in a mirror and one thing's sure; what we see is not who we are."

I have worked with thousands of clients throughout my career and one thing I have learned is that many look in the mirror and realize that their reflection does not make them happy. They are not satisfied with the image they see. Their reflection elicits pain and suffering. Some clients prefer to turn away from the mirror. What is it that is so repugnant that they turn away? What do they see? Is it a true reflection of their inner and outer beauty? Or is it a distorted view based on what we learned from messages that constantly are projected throughout our day and life?

Maybe you described an aspect of yourself when I asked who you are really. For example, you may have described your body (I am a svelte size 10), your personality (I am an optimist), or your favorite hobby (I am a surfboarder.)

Identity labels like these are useful, even necessary. They shape the way we act and feel (and the way people react to us) in every situation from taking the bus to choosing friends. However, many labels are misleading, and no one can fully describe the multifaceted reality that is a human being. Who you are reflects your core values, beliefs, personality and so much more. You are a product of your environment. However, who you are now can change. You can unleash your full potential and be the person you want to see in the mirror–and I am not talking about external appearance.

External labels are transitory not long lasting. They are fleeting and temporary. Nevertheless, the inner labels are the ones that bring us satisfaction, happiness, and well-being (a sense of serenity and fulfillment). These are permanent and long lasting. If we truly long for the real person in the mirror, then that person is the one evolving over time to become generous, kind, compassionate and gratuitous. That is someone to look at, admire and respect. This is a truly happy person.

Mini Morsel Sampling:

Look in the mirror; what you see is not who you are. So, now answer the question: who are you really? If time permits, cut out words and pictures from magazines that describe who you really are. Put them in a collage; refer to the words and pictures from time to time. Is that you? Who you are becoming?

Everything lately is done in record speed! We tend to jump on the treadmill of life and push until we drop. We aren't always sure if we digested words, instructions, or even our food because we gulp it down and move on. We microwave not only our food, but also our lives.

"We are in the process of microwaving; God is in the process of marinating."

But when we allow ourselves to *marinate*, what a difference! The taste is much more flavorful. The marinade awakens our senses. *Mini Morsel Sampling: So take time to marinate! Experiment with new flavors; explore challenging life events with curiosity. Where is life taking you as you adjust to the spices of being? What will you become? Write down your thoughts. Let them soak in. Slow down. Let God's marinade do its work.*

An Asset or a Liability? Who are you becoming?

When I hear the words *asset* and *liability*, my first thoughts are around banking or what is earned and owed. But when I think of those same words and connect them to who I am becoming, I wonder if I am

"For we must be one thing or the other, an asset or a liability, the sinew in your wing to help you soar, or the chain to bind you to earth."
Countee Cullen

an asset or a liability. If I am an asset, I am giving back or paying forward—being an agent of change. If I am a liability, I am taking from the world and not giving anything back. I am draining the people and resources around me. If I am an asset, I am investing in this world and in others creating opportunities. I am inspiring the community in which I live. That is real value. If I am a liability, I am robbing people, taking more and giving less. When I do that, I am not really happy. However, when I feel like I am truly an asset to the people and organizations that I am connected to, I know I am making a positive difference. I am making an impact. I am not hurting, but helping people. I am soaring high and not dragging myself along the earth—chained to the ground.

I don't know about you. But I want to be an asset not a liability. I believe that my personal net worth is of greater value and importance than even my financial net worth if I am an asset to society.

So who do you want to become? Do you want to be an asset or liability? Be the change!

Mini Morsel Sampling:

Where are you now? An asset or a liability? What steps can you take to improve your current performance and be more of an asset than a liability?

Chiseled Within

From teens to adults, we are inundated with societal messages captivated by the perfect chiseled bodies. We start quite early experimenting with latest diets, exercising trends, plastic surgeries, and all sorts of products that are designed to quickly eradicate lines, wrinkles, and cellulite. We are encouraged and determined to create a flawless image. Matter of fact, advertising makes it a point to capture that image. And, for most of us, it is impossible to attain. But we keep trying.

I understand the importance of exercise, eating healthy organic foods, and searching for advice on how to dress for success. I get caught up in the next marketing fad that promises the postponement of looking old. I sometimes envy the model that appears flawless.

I wonder, what will happen as we continue on life's journey if we only focus on molding our physiques; constantly seeking perfection? Often, we are left with a shell of a body.

I also am very aware that there is more to chisel away than just the outer layer of our bodies. We need to chisel within. We need to look deep at the other layers that make us who we are. We have to scrape away fears, phobias, prejudices, and habits that prevent us from learning about ourselves. How we can personally improve, prosper, and help others? We have to chip away at the rough edges of our personalities and our inner intolerances to grow and develop. And that isn't easy. It is sometimes painful.

But in order to cultivate the gem in us, we have to seek strategies and resources that continue to mold us into the person that we are becoming. We have to whittle away at our flaws. We have to cultivate positive performance behaviors to be the best person in a relationship, to attract the career we need to pursue. Then we can use retirement as a vehicle of expression instead of retreating from life in all its zest and adventure.

We all want to be *glittering diamonds* but often we resist being cut, to get to the jewel in us. Give yourself the permission to chisel away at the things that are holding you back. Instead of resisting, challenge yourself accepting the things you cannot change but consider the things that you can change; and those actions, thoughts, words will transform you. Have the courage to use your strengths and skills to confront personal change.

And, if you are seeking advice or ways to effectively mold your inner self into what you are to become, I can help you. Together, we can carefully cut away at the rough edges and discover the real you.

It can be an exciting time to chip away. You never know what you may uncover!

Mini Morsel Sampling:

Write down one thing that has been holding you back and challenge yourself to consider the thing you can change. Look at your strengths and underutilized talents. They are there to help and so am I.

Success, Mistakes and Failure

Bring on the mistakes!

It's easy to hold onto the mistakes we've made. It's easy to think of ourselves as ugly or broken or guilty or confused. We have the voices in our heads that remind us who we are not. We constantly compare ourselves to others, thinking we are less than perfect. Most of us make New Year commitments to change a poor behavior or to improve ourselves through personal development courses or reading. Maybe you are contemplating a new career and you are in the search process.

> "Failure is only a fact when you give up. Everyone gets knocked down, the question is: Will you get back up?"

However, I wonder if while attempting to make changes, you are afraid to make a mistake or fail. I have heard over and over again remarks such as these from clients "I am a failure!" "I just can't do it." "I am always giving up when things get tough." "I'll never amount to anything!"

Ah, those voices in our heads, they sound so convincing!

But, are those statements true?

What if we were to look at those mistakes and failures as an opportunity to learn, grow, and develop new strategies for coping and overcoming?

What if you adopted the Power of Intention as a way to learn from mistakes? What if today you manifested purposeful intentions to activate those intentions?

Wow! Just think who we could become?

According to Dr. Wayne Dyer "you get what you intend to create by being in harmony with the power of intention, which is responsible for all creation." Dr. Dyer proposes that we incorporate the 7 Faces of the Power of Intention which are be creative, be kind (to yourself too), love, be beauty, be ever expansive, be abundant (think and believe your life is abundant), and be receptive.

> ***Mini Morsel Sampling:***
>
> *So what are your intentions? How will you use the 7 Faces of the Power of Intention to shape and commit to a new way of being? What do your affirmations look like? How can you see past mistakes as lessons?*

Will you get back up?

We want to be perfect, not make mistakes and lose. Yet, there are times that we are not perfect. We make mistakes, and we lose. What do we learn from the imperfections, the blunder, and the losses?

When I opened my first personal training business in 1993, I was told that I would fail. Small businesses, I was reminded, fail within five years. I didn't believe that. I wouldn't accept it. So, I foraged ahead—determined to do things perfectly, without any oversight. The fact that I had researched the demographics for my community made me confident that my business would be successful.

How wrong I was! In the first six months, I was failing! My accountant informed me that if I didn't turn the business around immediately, I would be out of business. I needed a miracle. I felt beaten down. But only for a short time because, I re-evaluated what I was doing and I changed direction. I got back up on both feet and took giant steps forward. And, the business took an impressive turn; my accountant remarked that I had increased productivity by 120 percent!

I learned something important from this first bout of failure. I used failure as a way to learn and grow. I used failure as an opportunity to stretch my thinking and ignite my creative juices. These disasters presented challenges that could have knocked me down. I could have said "I give up." I could have seen myself as a disappointment. But, I bounced back up to prove that in spite of hard times, I could see the prize–I could win.

I look for failure to push me forward, to propel me to new places.

Mini Morsel Sampling:

So, what do you do when you get letdown? What do you do when you reach a plateau in your personal or business life? What do you do when you lose your job or loved one? What do you do when your business isn't producing results? Do you retreat or do you find ways to move forward? I'd like to know what you do and how you do it.

Athletes know about mental rehearsal, visualization, confidence and self-talk. They know these are powerful strength-building tools for winning and reaching their personal best or excellence.

Athletes know they have to believe it to become it. They have learned how to deal with stress because they have played their game physically, mentally, and spiritually. And they understand the importance of the mental practice; it is not enough to physically play well. The mind must actively work just as hard as the body.

> "It's not the winning that matters but the will to win."
> ~ Vince Lombardi

Athletes have the will to win; they have faced their fears and created a high level of self-confidence so that they can go out and challenge their opponents head-on. Athletes repeat what they need to hear in order to be confident, positive winners. While they may have some anxiety before a game, they can talk themselves into seeing a successful outcome. They know what to do; it is like a second nature to them.

We can learn from these techniques. I wanted to know why athletes could perform under stress, why they could win a race or game in spite of obstacles. We can learn from their will to win, their desire to succeed in spite of odds, and how they push themselves towards personal excellence. We need to encourage ourselves and our children to use these valuable techniques and be the winners they are called to be.

> ***Mini Morsel Sampling:***
>
> *What does your inner voice tell you about yourself when you make a mistake? Do you hear "I am a loser?" "I never get it right." "I am not as good as my teammates." What can you do as that inner critic tries to take control of your mind, body, and spirit? Find the other voice that tells the critical you that you are in charge; you are a winner. Remember when you got it right. Remember that feeling and the moment. And focus on being a good member of the team because you are. Each member of your team has their "down" moments so remember how you felt when you experienced negative self-talk. Then help each other find the positive memories of times they succeeded. Focus on that mental practice at home, sport, or school.*

Marilyn's Success Matrix

Everyone has a longing for meaning and purpose. Some recognize what that is immediately; others need some coaching.

A high level executive was searching for a new career, one that would bring her a sense of fulfillment. As she entered an unstable job market, she was forced to explore areas that would bring her financial and personal freedom. Her purpose, she learned, was also to stay on track for personal success and work on improving her health. Together, we co-created actions to explore and expand her strengths, skills, and talents as she evolves into the life she passionately wants.

Sometimes we are fully present, other times we are not. Once there is the recognition that there may be a conflict or an inner resistance to something and that is standing in our way, it prevents us from moving forward. There are some actions, thoughts, feelings—an inner voice that tells us that we are not good enough or smart enough to reach the results for which we are striving. As the coach for this executive we unleashed powerful thoughts and feelings to address what is holding her back. She now has strategies to incorporate while looking for a new career. She now has fun and the personal freedom to relax and restore.

Clients come in because they want something that they have not been able to achieve alone. A coach asks deep, powerful questions that evoke memories of the past which provide clues as to why we continue with our behaviors and stay stuck.

A woman, who came to me for weight loss initially, is moving into an area of interpersonal relationships with staff and superiors at work. She is creating some excellent actions or steps to engage her staff and supervisors to find solutions. She is learning to delegate. In her recent coaching session where she role played a situation and replayed the moment, she uncovered her inner resistance and she is now focused on taking care of herself and losing weight.

We all face challenges. Coaching helps clients respond to their challenges so that they are not paralyzed by them.

Feeling tremendously overwhelmed, another client contacted me to help her with her inability to move forward. Without realizing it, she had created a vicious cycle of overwhelmed, overeating, and overcompensating. We designed personal environments—people, places, ideas, and things that could provide her with the assets that she needed to overcome the major obstacles in her life.

We often feel like the way to accomplish something, is to make an inventory and mark it complete. There is little satisfaction in list-building. Often it is frustrating as the lists become longer. When I coach, I use recurring actions to help clients get to the results they want. For example, when one woman came to me for weight loss and we looked more closely at her lifestyle. As a film producer, she was on the road more than at home. Nutritious meals and working out were almost impossible for her to find and have time for. She felt that she had to do it all—being the mom, wife, and producer. Even when she was home, she stayed up late to finish laundry, the dishes, and her film projects. We co-created recurring actions that could make her home life easier so that she could find time for exercise, a warm bath, and more healthy dinners. We created actions that engaged the help of a housekeeper and her family so that she could take care of herself.

Tangible results are what I ask my clients to think about. How can we measure them? How can we hold you accountable? These results are always doable and take into account lifestyle and schedule. One client asked me to coach her because after her recent divorce, her teenage daughter became anorexic and belligerent. The client longed for family time, at least during dinner, where they could communicate without arguing. Because the daughter had a problem with anorexia, I suggested she seek the help of a psychotherapist for her daughter while I worked with the mom. Success was reached in several months after coaching!

Is what you are looking to achieve doable? Is it possible? That is one important ingredient that a coach uncovers in a coaching session. Whatever you long for must be designed in a way that you can reach it. As a child, I was told I would not amount to much. I had learning disabilities, difficulty with reading, and processing information. This belief strongly influenced my behavior toward learning until I realized that their perception of who I can become is only their opinion. I could believe them or change my belief. It was not easy to transform that belief—thoughts, feelings, and ideas are permanent reminders and need strategies to alter one's mindset. I believed I could win this battle and become a successful entrepreneur. I did that and I want you to believe that too!

> ### *Mini Morsel Sampling:*
>
> *What do you believe about yourself? Where did that belief come from? Is that credence true or false? How can you design a new acceptance of yourself without the interference of other's opinions?*

Living Life

PERSPECTIVE!

I clearly remember the years I spent as a media specialist for the Bedford School District in Bedford, NY producing in-house cable videos for the public school district and its surrounding community. It gave me great joy to find talent, interview guests before airtime, set up cameras for the studio shoot, and record interesting local news. What I really loved though was to go to the live location and videotape plays, concerts, games and other school-related events. Then I would go back to the editing suite and spend countless hours to create a complete television production with slides, graphics and music. It was delightful to witness the outcome of each show and its positive reaction from the cable viewers.

> "Be fearless in the pursuit of what sets your life on fire."

I guess I had the most fun shooting images from every possible angle. I captured scenes of the performance, concert, or school events from all distinctive aspects.

I chose every shooting angle imaginable. I would film in rain, sun, snow, and in all kinds of weather trying to capture the light, darkness, the dancing snowflakes, and hard pellets of rain that might suddenly appear within a moment's notice. I videotaped through tall grasses, around trees, through fences trying to approach images from a different outlook.

In the editing suite, I noticed with awe how the same picture or story shot at a different angle could produce dissimilar interpretations. And if I altered the photo shoot using various editing techniques, the perspective of the view would also change to reflect the latest film interpretation.

I learned something in that editing room and in constructing a story to tell. It is easy to see your perspective and believe in its right point of view but it is far better to see things at a unique angle, —because you may discover there is another way to see the same picture from a different position.

It just depends on your point of view—your perspective!

> ***Mini Morsel Sampling:***
>
> *Instead of jumping to conclusions about something or someone, put yourself in their shoes. Look at the situation from their perspective. You might see things differently. Each of you may be right in your viewpoint. How can this incident be a win-win for both sides when they clearly have seen something from a different perspective? What has changed? Moving forward, what will you remember as a takeaway?*

NO LIMITS

What are you doing to reach your full potential? You may not realize it but you have the power to change your perceptions of what you believe you can achieve, and be a winner! Whoever you are, whatever you do for a living, you can change your story and align positive emotions to attract the things that will make you more successful. First, you need a mental shift—you need to believe that your wish is your command.

If you are feeling stuck, or feeling like you are unlucky in business or life, what are you doing to get out of that mental pothole? What action steps are you taking to be the winner you were meant to be? You may be working on an advertising campaign, networking with community members, speaking on a regular basis, and attending conferences. You may be writing books, sending out monthly newsletters, producing audiotapes and video testimonials. You may be doing a variety of great things! However, you are missing one thing—visualizing your future as successful!

I am going to tell you a true story before I give you practical ways to visualize your possibilities. There once was a fighter pilot. On a particular aircraft mission, his plane crashed. After being airlifted to a nearby hospital, this man was told by his doctor that he was paralyzed from the neck down and that he would be on a respirator for the rest of his life. All he could do to communicate was blink his eyes.

The only thing he had was the power of his mind. You see, he believed that his thoughts can become things and that when you focus on what you want, you get it! So, he visualized breathing on his own. Every day, he saw himself breathing without the respirator; and within months, the respirator was removed! Now, the man whose spinal cord had been damaged imagined himself walking out of the hospital. He gave himself a specific time frame—of two years. Each day, he saw himself getting out of the hospital bed, feet making contact with the floor, gradually straightening his spine, and moving toward the front door of his room. In two years, this man walked slowly out of the door as he had imagined! A miracle that shows there is no limit to the wishes the universe will grant us—if only we will allow it!

Have you ever wondered why when things are going wrong in a day, several more negative things happen? It's as if when one bad thing occurs, several unpleasant things follow. When that happens, we are actually allowing negative thoughts and emotions to control us. Don't believe me? Try changing your beliefs. Shift your awareness towards more positive emotions—push aside any negative or self-defeating thoughts. Good thoughts attract good thoughts. We are like magnets and the universe will send us what we ask for and there are no limits to your wishes —your wish is your command.

Mini Morsel Sampling:

Visualizing your possibilities is a process. List on a piece of paper what you are grateful for, and then visualize it. See whatever you are visualizing as it already happened. Visualization takes time; so do not expect results after one try. It takes practice, concentrate, and emphatic belief. You can create vision boards—pictures of what you envision happening. Personal trainers often tell clients to picture their muscles working or imagine how they will look ten pounds thinner. Again, whatever you do for a living, you must decide on what you want, believe it, and say you deserve it! If you want more money, see it coming easily and say, "I am so happy and grateful to have $20,000 in gross monthly revenues." If you want several offices, gyms, or studios, picture with gratitude how they will look, when they will come into being. Envision the *interior of the buildings, the texture of the walls, the floors patterns, the lighting, the furniture, and the equipment. Smell the richness of the furniture in the reception area and hear the sounds of the phones ringing off the hook. Say "I am so happy and grateful to have one office per year, three studios in two years. I am so happy and grateful that the gross revenues exceed (put an amount in there) per month." Ask what you want several times a day and mean it! Never hesitate! Ask, believe, and you will receive!*

You can even use symbols to help you remember attitude with gratitude. One man used a small smooth stone as a symbol to remind him each day to be more positive and grateful. It was an ordinary stone, one found in his backyard brook. He placed this polished, grey stone on his dresser; and each morning when he picked it up, he said aloud those things he was thankful for—even those things that had not come into fruition, but what he could foresee or imagine happening. Then he put the stone in his pocket to carry with him during the day as a reminder to be grateful each and every moment. When he arrived home at night, he took it out of his pocket and as he put it on his bedroom dresser, he once again said aloud what he was grateful for—seeing it vividly and without doubt. Several months later, this man was with a friend visiting him from Africa. All of a sudden, as the man reached in his pocket for his wallet, his stone fell onto the ground.

The visitor asked what was the significance of the stone and why was he carrying it with him? The visitor was told that it was his *gratitude stone.* He further elaborated on ways the stone changed his life for the better. When the visitor returned home to Africa, he found his young son nearing death. The visitor immediately wired his friend in the states and asked for the gratitude stone—having listened to his friend's stories of the stone's great healing powers. His friend sent the stone to his African friend and within two months, a letter arrived from Africa. The letter described how after receiving the stone from his friend, his son's health completely changed—and now his son, was no longer at death's door and was healed. The stone held no power—but the mind did!

So, what does this mean for you? Dr. Denis Waitley, author of *The Psychology of Winning*, says that to be a winner **attitude is the answer**. He continues, "Your attitude towards your potential is either the **key to** or the **lock on** the door of personal fulfillment." I believe that in order for you to fully reach your potential and realize your dreams, you must first shake free all those negative, self-depreciating thoughts about yourself.

Mini Morsel Sampling:

You need to create and re-shape your life story. Don't focus on past events but project a grateful attitude towards all those things that will come to you, which you deserve. See clearly by visualizing all the possibilities that are coming your way. Invite the universe in, align yourself with it, and become what you think about. And, if you become what you think about, you will do amazing things and be more successful! Remember: what the mind conceives, the body achieves! There are no limits!

It's not about losing weight...it's about gaining Life!

"I've missed over nine thousand shots in my career. I've lost almost three hundred games. Twenty-six times, I've been trusted to take the game-winning shot and I have missed. I've failed over and over and over again in my life. And that is why I succeed." *Michael Jordan Professional Basketball Player*

Over the past 18 years, I have worked with clients who specifically wanted to lose weight. Some people had a little weight to lose; some wanted to lose a lot of weight. They often came to me frustrated saying that they either hit a plateau in their weight loss journey or felt like their goal was impossible to achieve. They tried every diet plan and exercise program. They joined a gym, hired a nutritionist, and tried hypnotism. And some bought the latest piece of equipment advertised on late night television. They spent precious time, money, and energy and came up with the end result but none of these weight loss programs were sustainable. Either the packaged food was repulsive, the exercise program painful, or some part of the process was highly unachievable long term.

What I learned in working with clients is that they believe that their weight loss failure is inevitable and that they will never succeed. They think that they are destined to fail over and over again. If they miss their mark (weight loss in pounds for the week), they give up, retreat, and go back to their old eating and exercise habits. They are unaware that out of failure comes success. Weight struggles are *doorway symptoms*–conditions leading us deeper into our life, our journey, and ourselves. We are on a journey of self-discovery, self-acceptance, and self-nourishment. If we do not fail, even with our weight, we will never know how to be more aware in life or how to listen to the wisdom of our body.

Missing over and over again is OK; as long as we learn from the missing. Your body is taking you on a personal journey, giving you time to reflect and discover yourself. Weight loss is not about losing weight...it's about gaining life!

Mini Morsel Sampling:

Your goal may not be to lose weight. Whatever the objective is, focus on how the end result will change and shape you. Your purpose will change periodically, so will the discovery of how you are gaining life.

"Play enthusiastically throughout your life!"

Do you remember the expression "All work and no play make Jack a dull boy?" That may refer to children but I believe it refers to adults too!

Remember recess? Remember when you played hide and seek, tag, and red rover, red rover? Remember when you jumped rope or built forts, or played with dolls or dressed up as an imaginary character?

We all know children need play time. Lack of play affects emotional development, leading to the rise of anxiety, depression, and problems of attention as well as self-control.

> "What do most Nobel Laureates, innovative entrepreneurs, artists; well-adjusted children, happy couples and families, and the most successfully adapted mammals have in common? They play enthusiastically throughout their lives."
> Stuart Brown, Institute of Play

But what about adults—do they need recess? Do they require play time too? I am of the strong opinion that we have encouraged the decline of children's free play since around 1955. As adults, we have exerted increasing control over children's activities. Author Peter Gray,

Ph.D., Professor of Psychology (emeritus) at Boston College defines "free play" as play that a child undertakes, which is self-directed and an end in itself, rather than a part of an organized activity. This type of play is a testing ground for life. Play is critical for developing self-confidence, for connecting to one's self-identified and self-guided interests. Play helps with decision making, problem solving, and the ability to follow rules. Children learn how to handle their emotions, including anger and fear during play. Play also helps children make friends and learn how to get along with others as equals. Most importantly, play is a source of happiness. The loss of play gives rise to anxiety and depression.

Do you see why adults need to incorporate play into their lives? Play enthusiastically throughout your life!

Mini Morsel Sampling:

Find ways at work, home or school to play. List three habits that you can integrate during the day that will be pleasurable and playful. Try a little playtime. How does that make you feel?

Life Begins At 40!

Are you forty yet? If you are or if you are approaching the dreaded forty, fifty, or even seventy year old mark, have you ever thought that you could still train for longevity? Start right this minute to get healthy and fit for the rest of your life! Do you think it possible?

Let me ask you a question: What are you willing to start doing today? Begin with something small but get going!

I remember looking at a picture of a woman lifting a heavy power bar. How old is she, I wondered? Was she forty, fifty, sixty, or seventy years old? Did it matter that I know? Whatever her age, I thought, she is obviously training for longevity. Clearly she was not in her teens, twenties, thirties or forties. What an inspiration for our youth! And what an inspiration for all adults over fifty years old! It is never too late to start exercising.

I started weight training at forty. I was overweight and asthmatic. I began the exercise program to lose weight but most important to get fit. I needed to drastically change my sedentary lifestyle and eat healthy foods. And once I started, I began to feel different. I liked who I was. I felt more confident. And, I happily no longer needed inhalers! Asthma under control and weight loss was results of my efforts. I was hooked!

Maybe, you may never be able to lift like the woman I described (maybe you will) that may not be your goal—it wasn't mine. But if you could maintain your independence for as long as you can–lifting groceries, bags of fertilizer and dog food, playing with grandchildren, and just doing things you always enjoyed doing—like skiing, tennis, running, swimming and dancing? What would that mean to you?

So, if this is something you value—your independence, what are you willing to do, especially after forty, to live your life fully? Are you willing to consider choosing better nourishing foods, increasing your daily fitness routine, decreasing your stress, increasing the amount and quality of your sleep?

At forty do we begin to get hints of our mortality? Did something happen to us— a wakeup call or a symptom of an illness that tells us that we need to take care of our bodies, minds, and emotions better?

When I was little, I watched my grandparents and great grandparents (one of whom lived to the age of one-hundred and four and never went to the doctor) really live life to the fullest. They trained for longevity at every age. They cooked gardened, cleaned, sewed, played outdoor games, danced and played instruments. They didn't entertain conversations about the difficulties of getting older. They seemed to focus on providing their families with nutritious foods, spiritual guidance or faith, emotional support, fun activities that reduced stress and encouraged social support. Age was only a number; biologically each person was as young as they felt.

Probably the most famous senior athlete was Jack Lalanne. Jack was a well-known fitness and bodybuilding expert; a motivational speaker well into his nineties. The fit senior citizen famously once said:

"I train like I'm training for the Olympics or for a Mr. America contest, the way I've always trained my whole life. You see, life is a battlefield. Life is survival of the fittest. How many healthy people do you know? How many happy people do you know? Think about it. People work at dying, they don't work at living. My workout is my obligation to life. It's my tranquilizer. It's part other way I tell the truth — and telling the truth is what's kept me going all these years."

Mini Morsel Sampling:

For Jack and many fit seniors, life didn't begin at forty. They were always living, training, actively involved, doing things they were passionate about, being happy, sharing joy, leaving a legacy, and imparting their wisdom. But for some of you who have not begun living and are approaching a big birthday, let me ask you this: What's preventing you from beginning today? What would your life look like if you were really living?

Life Stinks!

Yesterday, I stayed cool by watching a movie starring Mel Brooks. The title of it was *Life Stinks*! I chose it because I love comedy and needed a laugh. But I was very surprised at how little I laughed!

You see, the movie is about a very filthy rich businessman who bets a corporate rival that he can live on the streets of L.A. without the comforts of home or money, which proves to be tougher than he thought.

In the movie, Mel led a luxurious life. It was opulent with expensive clothes, artwork, mansion, and a limo–all to impress. Even the people who worked for him shared the same attitude to impress and disassociated themselves from the suffering and homelessness around them. Mel was used to paying people for services, paying people off, when necessary to get what he wanted.

Out on the street, Mel was forced to fend for himself, he was beaten, reduced to eat in soup kitchens, and constantly on the move because his cardboard home was flooded by inclement weather or set on fire by vagrants and drug addicts. Mel quickly learned that life on the streets literally stinks! Few people genuinely cared or offered assistance. Street people were invisible. When one of Mel's friends collapsed and died in front of a shopkeeper's store, the shopkeeper only cared that his business would be interrupted by a dead man, outside his restaurant door. He was not concerned about this man's condition or his death. There was no empathy for the deceased.

While this new life was not easy for Mel and his new friends, he learned something that out of the *stink* of life, there is beauty and purpose. He learned that there are moments of happiness and joy; and that each moment should be treasured and appreciated. Mel also learned that there is strength that comes out of the conviction to stand up for yourself, believe in your abilities, and confidently change the system. If Mel had not experienced the stench of life, he would never have smelled the "sweetness" that comes about with inner transformation. He would have not learned compassion for others or sought to use what he learned to benefit the people who needed permanent housing, the homeless. In the end, Mel overcame all odds and built a new community for the homeless.

Mini Morsel Sampling:

So, if life stinks for you, what are you willingly to do about it? What are you willing to do in order to change it and make it smell better?

A Motion for Mercy

I promise this day to show...

- Compassion instead of coldness
- Pity instead of blame
- Clemency instead of heartlessness
- Forgiveness instead of ruthlessness
- Kindness instead of cruelty
- Sympathy instead of a lack of understanding
- Humanity instead of inhumanity
- Understanding instead of indifference
- Generosity instead of miserliness
- Leniency instead of severity
- Benevolence instead of spitefulness
- Forbearance instead of impatience
- Grace instead of unkindness

Because the world is in need of mercy, it has to start with me. It is my motion for mercy!

Mini Morsel Sampling:

Which trait will you choose today to act upon?

Empowerment

"It's what's between your ears that counts."

I like this maxim because it reminds me to consider what I think or believe in because, my thoughts shape my outcome. If I think negatively, my mind will naturally attract destructive results. I have seen that happen to me and my coaching clients.

"It took quite a long time to develop a voice and now that I have it, I am not going to be silent." Madeline

If I persist to believe that my past controls my future then the consequence will be just no opportunity and no chance to reach my full potential. I will remain in a vacuum fashioned by the abyss of my own thoughts and beliefs.

If I allow other people to tell me who I am and what I am capable of, then I am giving others the permission to make the choices for me. For example, when I was a child I had undiagnosed dyslexia. My reading was adequate but my comprehension was poor. I had difficulty in grasping certain concepts, especially mathematical formulas. Instead of helping me understand what I needed to do to improve, I was told I was slow and that there was no way I could go to college. I began to see myself as a failure. School and studying was synonymous with defeat. Physically, I became ill suffering from stomach aches and migraines. Mentally, I felt unworthy, unlovable, and lacked a healthy self-image. I truly believed that I would never amount to anything.

Until one day, for some reason, I became angry. I was angry with the stories about myself that were not written by me! I decided to stop believing *what was between my ears*. Those stories lead to defeat and destruction. So, I didn't learn like other kids in my class, but there were things I could learn. I would focus on the skills and talents that I had. I would learn to express them even though I was scared to death. My new story between my ears brought me confidence, creativity, resiliency, and wisdom. I was in charge of my fate.

Stories are wonderful. As the author, you have the power to write the middle and the end as long as you believe *it's what's between your ears that counts* and you can take the **action** to do something about your beliefs.

"Knowledge is not power, applied knowledge is power!"

I started my career after receiving a Master's degree in Education. I always felt that knowledge was power, and anyone could rise up and free themselves from a current life situation through education and knowledge.

You see after I left education to open a fitness business, I applied my teaching skills to my new career. My clients, a bit like my former high school students, needed to be taught lessons on healthy eating and stimulating exercises. My clients again like my former students came prepared for their lessons but often did not apply them after our sessions together. It was most disheartening, not only for me but also for my clients. You see, most of them had a goal and they could not seem to sustain or obtain their goal. They had the knowledge, but they did not apply it.

I wondered how I could take the knowledge and help them design actions that would allow them to apply that knowledge in a fun and challenging way. As a former teacher, a personal trainer, entrepreneur, now a positive performance coach with an Applied Sports Psychology degree, I know that providing health screenings, assessments, and education is not enough. Knowledge is important; more important is applying knowledge to make the mind shift for that alternative lifestyle behavior you are seeking.

> **Mini Morsel Sampling:**
>
> *What one thing can you do today to make that mind shift?*

Recently, I have been reading articles about losing weight and getting paid to do it. It is an interesting proposition.

I never really entertained being part of a weight loss contest with a cash reward at the end of the game. But with the advent of television shows like *The Biggest Loser* where contestants who failed in the past to lose weight join other folks like themselves, paying to lose weight might not be a bad idea. Dangling a prize to *win to lose* seems like fun idea; although on this TV show, watching contestants' pained expressions, cries of agony, and abusive treatment from their trainers makes me wonder if it is worth losing weight even if there is a prize at the end.

> "Money is only a tool. It will take you wherever you wish, but it will not replace you as the driver."
> ~Ayn Rand

I used a weight loss game with clients who wanted to lose weight. I paired people into small groups. These buddies chose their team name, they cheered each other on, they weighed in together, and gave each other tips for meal planning and exercising. Eventually, a team won! It was exciting. Rewards were handled out.

However, shortly after the prize was accepted, these same contestants went back to their old habits. Their reward was a gimmick. It got them their result but it did not change their behaviors. It did not replace the driver.

You see, you are the driver. You sit behind the steering wheel of your own life. You can decide which way to turn. You can choose to go forward or put your life in reverse. You can drive to your goal, especially if you are offered a very tempting prize. But, once you get to your destination (your goal) if you haven't replaced what's driving you and if you haven't changed the internal mechanism that pushes you, then the money or prize hasn't taught you anything.

You are still the same driver; money is only a tool.

Mini Morsel Sampling:

If you want to change the way you drive and you have purchased my book, I want to offer you a forty minute free session with me to uncover those tools.

Anger and the Tongue

Ten Ways to Continue Doing What you're doing to Stay Angry

1. Surround yourself with like-minded angry people
2. Invest all your time and energy focusing on how you think someone wronged you
3. Share the wrongdoings with as many people as you can
4. Recount all the negative things people have done to you
5. Carefully weigh how much you do and how little others do

"The tongue is but a small, soft flesh. Yet, it is capable of breaking the strongest bonds and destroying the most powerful of relationships."
Yasir Quadir

6. Forget the good things that were done to you or by others you love
7. Justify your anger by creating stories that help keep you in control
8. Focus on how to punish rather than forgive
9. Hold on to your justifiable anger for as long as you can until you become bitter
10. Savor the taste of anger swallowing its poisonous venom for as long as you can

The result: you become a bitter, angry person with manifestations of physical illness.

Mini Morsel Sampling:

Let me help you gain a better perspective on what is behind your anger and techniques to manage anger better. I will give you a 40 minute free anger management session after purchasing my book.

MINI MORSEL 18

Forgiveness and Mercy

You cannot do a kindness too soon, for you never know how soon it will be too late.

It's never too late to learn to read, to build an empire or to follow a dream or passion.

It's never too late to play a game, to smile at a stranger, to encourage the disheartened or to change a career.

It's never too late to start a family, to love again or to start discovering you.

"Without forgiveness life is governed by an endless cycle of resentment and retaliation."
Roberto Assagioli

It's never too late to find joy, bring joy, or foster friendships.

It's never too late to start exercising, to sleep late, relax more, or to find some balance.

It's never too late to write a book, to overcome an obstacle or fear, to quit smoking, to be inspired or to change your mind.

It's never too late to give up our prejudices, to forgive those who hurt us, to explore our heartfelt desires, or to find our higher calling or purpose.

It's never too late to leave a legacy, to learn how to play a sport, to sign up for dance lessons or to tell a joke.

It's never too late to touch a life by doing a good deed or show an act of kindness without expecting anything in return.

- It's never too late to apologize.
- It's never too late to forgive.
- You have today.
- What if tomorrow were too late?

Mini Morsel Sampling:

What are doing today to ensure that tomorrow is not too late?

.

More or Less

My Tree House

was probably around eight years old when my dad moved us into our brand new home. He worked long hours to construct that house in the suburbs. My parents found a

"Live simply. Give more. Expect less." Rita Zahara

picture of a home they loved, bought the plans, and the land; then set their sights on planning and designing their perfect home. Using recycled windows and barn wood from dad's family furniture store, dad sawed the wood; hammered nails each evening after spending long hours of laying the linoleum tiles and wall-to-wall carpeting in customer's houses. He endured long nights, until the wee hours of the morning-- painstakingly and lovingly constructing the furniture for our home and a large bar downstairs in the family room with a brass footrest along its bottom. It was so modern having a small refrigerator and sink where the bartender could stand and serve. Dad was so talented. I loved watching him—delighted in observing the way he handcrafted pieces of furniture or fixed broken appliances. I remember he built a wooden bench for our family room that opened to reveal a place to store blankets or books. On the surface Mom placed a colorful cushion to make it more comfortable to sit on.

I would appear in his basement workroom to watch and help—handing him tools and just talking. I was fascinated by my dad's creative abilities. He had little schooling as his own dad died when he was a young man. So, abruptly his calling in life was to aid his brothers and sister run the family business.

I think about the sacrifices that Dad made. I never heard him complain that his life wasn't fair. He appreciated life and loved music, laughter, and family. He was always there for family.

When we finally moved into our beautiful home, it featured three bedrooms, a large kitchen, two full bathrooms, and two half baths; a far cry from our one bedroom apartment over a bar in town. Four of us shared the old bedroom and one bathroom. We also shared the flat with rats. Now, we were blessed with a home on one acre of property! We had a chance to climb trees and roll carelessly down hills. We played in the woods and watched nature at her finest. No more playing behind the bar underneath our apartment.

When I think of my dad who I miss so much, I also think of our tree house, the one he built from scratch, modeled after our home. The roof lines pitched like our home, the expansive windows—a replica of our home's windows. This wasn't a tree house made out of wood and haphazardly plopped in a tree; but our tree house stood majestically on large posts cemented to the ground. It featured screens on the windows and a ladder leading up to our entry—a trap door! That tree house was the best gift from dad ever. Mom created picnic lunches and often my brother and I ascended to our retreat where we could imagine and dream of our future.

I think of my dad with such gratitude and love.

Mini Morsel Sampling:

Think about this: what kind of love do you give? How do you build your love? Conditionally? Unconditionally? How would you like to receive love in return?

Less is more

December is the time of year when we seem to want more stuff!

I just went out yesterday afternoon for a drive and I could not believe the parking lots filled with cars. I haven't seen that many cars in a while. Stores opened their doors a little earlier than years prior to accommodate buyers. If you watched the news, you saw that consumers were busy filling up their shopping carts with the best bargains they could get for the holiday season.

So, what's the purpose of more? Does it fill us up? Does it truly satisfy? Or does it make us want more? It seems that more is addictive. If we have more, we want more and we will do anything to get more. And, if you have more, we think that we will feel more abundant, content, and fulfilled.

Yet, I can recall a time when I had less but felt as if I had much more. Perhaps we should all ask ourselves how we can live our lives more fully and abundantly without more.

> The greatest wealth is health.
> ~Virgil

Mini Morsel Sampling:

Let me know how you are living your life with less and feeling as if you had more! I would love you to share your stories with me.

My mother always told me that health is wealth. She reminded me often that if you have your health, you have everything. I didn't realize how powerful a statement it was until I became an adult. Because, as a child, you feel like you are invincible. Even in your twenties and thirties, you still feel that the illness of age or the constant barrage of physical misuse to the body (like drugs and alcohol) will somehow not find you and make you sick. You believe you will continue to survive. And, perhaps you do, to an extent.

When you see the preponderance of genetically modified and processed foods that is prevalent today, we are walking around like the living dead. We continue to eat poorly, exercise or move sporadically, if not at all, and we drink in great quantities substances that dull our senses and sedate our restless souls. We allow stress to destroy our consciousness or mindfulness, avoiding the positive steps we can take to reduce our anxiety and fear. Instead we create urgency about everything we must do forgetting the things we could do to make us happier and really fulfilled.

Health is definitely wealth. There was time in my life when I was quite ill. It caused depression and anxiety. I suffered through many medical treatments until I decided to take responsibility for my own actions and chose to make healthy choices in my own life. I have also seen people around me—friends and family become quite debilitated by disease, especially cancer. It has opened my eyes to choose prevention—intentionally educating myself on nourishing the body with wholesome, organic foods and feeding my mind and soul with optimistic intentions and affirmations. Being prosperous and having accumulated power, money, and fame is fine but it still brings us nothing in the end if we are fed medicines and pills, stuck in bed; in an attempt to restore our health.

Mini Morsel Sampling:

I wonder if I could challenge you today to start creating a healthy environment for yourself. What would that look like for you? What small steps can you take to change the way you are living right now? How can you move from the living dead to living alive, fully conscious, and truly wealthy? I'd love to hear your thoughts.

Richer than the Donald

Recently I ran into a friend I hadn't seen in a while. We exchanged pleasantries; then I asked how his business was doing. He sighed, and then said "OK. But I'm not getting rich." I replied "You are already rich!"

It is amazing to me how much we rely on our financial investments, our savings, and other accumulated wealth and accoutrements to paint a picture of how prosperous we are. It concerns me that we are impressed by people who say they are loaded with dough but maybe penniless in the treasures of the world that money cannot buy.

I don't have to brag about the car I own, the house I work hard to keep, the paltry vacations I take, the clothing I choose to purchase, or the people who I say love me so much.

What I do have to boast about is the blessings I already have like my friends, job, and health. I am rich in fitness and coaching affiliations plus social causes that impact all of us. I am connected with matters that concern our community, country, and world. I am blessed by the strangers I meet each day—their conversations enrich my life! I am rich in spirit, in mercy, and forgiveness. I am well off each night for the food on my plate and the ability to worship in peace.

You may think you can buy things and that will give you fulfillment and happiness. However, how many times do you get what you want and feel empty desiring more? The things in life that give you satisfaction and joy are investing in others before yourself and in forgiving which is the highest form of love.

I may not have vast hordes of money in my bank accounts but I am rich beyond my wildest dreams. I really believe I am richer than the Donald. How affluent are you?

> ***Mini Morsel Sampling:***
>
> *And, if you are looking to get rich in the things money cannot buy, I can help you find your blessings; together we can count them, and see how wealthy you really are in this moment and how much more affluent you can be in the future. If you are unsure about your current and potential wealth, then contact me for a forty minute free wealthy consultation.*

Weave Magi Magic

During the month of December, I am reminded of the wonderful tale by O. Henry *The Gift of the Magi*. If you have not read this short story, then I suggest you do. If you have read it, I ask that you revisit it. It may change how you weave your Magi gifts this holiday season.

In O. Henry's story, Della and Jim, husband and wife, were quite poor. This particular Christmas, they had $1.87 in the wallet—not enough money with which to purchase presents for each other. Yet they found unselfish ways to part with what they considered dear to them in order to magically produce gifts for each other on Christmas Eve.

Both Della and Jim owned irreplaceable possessions. Della had the most lustrous, long hair; it was her pride and joy. Her brown hair cascaded almost to her knees. Jim possessed a gold watch that had been his father's and grandfather's, he treasured it for sentimental reasons so saying goodbye to it would be difficult. Yet, Della and Jim made quiet, secretive decisions to sell their treasures in order to make each other's holiday special.

Della visited Sofronie's shop *Hair Goods of All Kinds* and inquired how much the madam would pay Della for her long hair. She was offered $20 and without hesitation, Della ordered the salon owner to cut her hair. With her newly found cash, Della looked for the perfect gift for Jim—a beautiful platinum fob chain for his beloved watch.

Jim, on the other hand, who had no gloves and wore a torn overcoat, sold his priceless watch for a set of combs, =that Della had worshipped long in a Broadway window. They were beautiful combs, pure tortoise shell, with jeweled rims.

The story ends, with a moral about making sacrifices— unbelievable losses to provide valuable gifts to loved one.

I am also reminded about the story of the three wise men, the Magi who walked afar following a star to give three priceless gifts to someone they did not know, someone they heard about—a king.

Della and Jim were married to each other; their love was unconditional. The Magi, on the other hand, did not know who they were really going to visit. They heard a rumor, followed their instincts and sacrificed their gifts of gold, frankincense, and myrrh (practical gifts) — gold as a precious metal, frankincense as perfume or incense, and myrrh as anointing oil. They gave their gifts to an unknown king. Della and Jim's gifts did not turn out to be practical but in their foolish giving, they realized how much each person was willing to let go of the things they valued in order to make the other person happy.

It is easy to make sacrifices for the people we love and know—and give impractical, foolish gifts. Maybe it's not so easy to give a precious, practical gift to someone we do not know.

Mini Morsel Sampling:

So, I am challenging you to make a sacrifice and give something precious and practical not only to someone you know and love but also to someone you may not know. Let's weave Magi magic in the life of another. Take it from me, you will find joy and happiness in the giving.

Love

"The greatest thing you'll ever learn is to love and be loved in return."

Unforgettable with Love by Natalie Cole

"I love you for all that you are, all that you have been, and all that you're meant to be."

Love sometimes hurts. Love hurts so good and so bad. However, without love, I do believe that we are incapable of growing. Like a tree, we sometimes need pruning and re-shaping. Sure, it hurts to be pruned; although when the trimming is finished, we may feel tremendous joy at our new appearance.

As Kahlil Gibran says in his poetic book *The Prophet*, "love's ways are hard and steep; his voice may shatter your dreams. As love crowns you so shall he crucify you." Who, then, is not familiar with love's pleasures and pains? I think we all share the same joys and sorrows, in loving.

I am thankful for each day I can love...family, friends and strangers because love makes my day amazing, and to those for whom I have loved but are no longer here, their indelible tenderness is still imprinted on my heart.

Mini Morsel Sampling:

Who do you thank for another day of loving! And how can you make someone feel loved? What can you do now?

The Heart Whisperer

During the month of February, most of us think about love, appreciation for family, friends, neighbors, and pets. We want to surprise our loved ones with thoughtful gifts, gestures that remind us of the past, and signs of the possibilities that the future holds for all of us.

With tenderness, we give our hearts to others because of Valentine's Day; partly because it is also the Heart Health Month. We send cards, candy, flowers and demonstrate expressions of kindness as a Valentine's Day expression. We are reminded through various media advertisements how important diet and exercise are, if we want to keep our hearts healthy.

It may be impossible to love ourselves and others unconditionally. It may be risky and pointless to try to understand the humanness of one another. Yet, our whispering heart, if we listen to its quiet, pulsating, rhythmic beats calls out to us saying "Give it a try."

We may choose to call ourselves heart whisperers this month, but if we truly are the transmitters of heart health and healing, do we show affection to those near and dear to us? What about other people unlike us (or perhaps just like us only we do not recognize ourselves in the others)?

In light of what our global community is enduring, the pointless suffering, the inhumanity to men, women and children across every gender, creed, ethnicity, and religion, is it really risky, or pointless to cast our differences aside and notice our similarities?

If we are heart whisperers, then all we have to do is *give it a try*. Hear your heart whisper, listen to its love beating and send whispers of kind-heartedness to all with whom you come into contact with not just for the month of February.

Mini Morsel Sampling:

How can you personally make a difference in your community? What small act of kindness is possible for you to do each day? You will discover that love creates joy and peace when you give more love away.

Values

The World

The world is a terrible place. It's easy to feel that way. We are seeing unbridled weather-related storms that devastate different areas of the world, leaving hundreds of people homeless. We are witnessing unparalleled outbreaks of gun violence even against children. Domestic bloodshed

> "I stand for honesty, equality, kindness, compassion, treating people the way you want to be treated, and helping those in need. To me, those are traditional values."

is on the rise. Hostility against races, ethnicities, gender, and sexual orientation blatantly continues. Wars last indefinitely; terrorism's intensity and savagery almost appears normal. Even driving cars on highways or country back roads are equally dangerous, as road rage seems to be increasing. So, as we add up the atrocities against the environment and its people, the world can be seen as a terrible place.

As Americans begin to celebrate their freedom (their independence day is on the 4th of July) I would ask you to think about what freedom means to you. Yes, we live in a free country, thanks to the men and women who fought and continue to fight for liberty, justice, and the pursuit of happiness. I wonder are we willing to choose to protect, **rather than neglect our world, our country, our people, and all people from all backgrounds. I wonder if we are willing to carefully choose our thoughts, our actions, our words and the delivery of those words. How does what we say and what we do affect others? What would that look like? We might create the freedom that I believe we all deserve.**

You may think you have to do something big, something that takes a lot of time to show that you care. However, something small can be huge, like a smiling at a stranger, or not speeding and cutting someone off and then giving them the finger. You can give by not expecting anything in return and showing someone the respect they deserve. You can celebrate your freedom by thanking the men and women who are making it possible for you to be at home safe and secure. You can celebrate your freedom by making sure everyone enjoys the same freedoms. You can let go of your prejudices, abusive behavior, small talk, petty obsession with possessions and perfect looks.

Maybe if we all did something small to show that we care, the world might not be such a terrible place. Maybe we can create a future for our children that models behaviors of decency, respect, love of country and all the principles that our fore founders struggled to establish.

Mini Morsel Sampling:

How will you cherish and protect our rights by caring to change how we treat our environment, our country, its citizens, and the citizens of the world?

I've been in business for over seventeen years. I love being the innovator of new ideas, creating and marketing products that I feel my clients really desire. Health and fitness with an emphasis on wellness and positive performance coaching.

"People are definitely a company's greatest asset. It doesn't make any difference whether the product is cars or cosmetics. A company is only as good as the people it keeps."
– Mary Kay Ash

When I started my fitness business (and now my coaching practice), I knew I needed principles or standards for my team to follow. These principles were the basis of our tribal culture, our language, dress, attitude, demeanor, and thinking needed to be consistent with my company's philosophy. The standards created reflected core values that align with my purpose and passion: respect for the individual, honesty and integrity in building relationships, and teamwork! My *tribe* (my people who share similar beliefs and values) was expected to work together respectfully and honestly. I stressed to the team that they must focus on quality through excellence and support through community. And my door was always open to listen and support my team and clients.

While my guiding principles were tremendously important, equally essential were the products and the services provided; they go hand in hand. However, from years of experience, I have learned that people (my tribe) are my greatest asset. Without the right combination of people all rooting together for the common goal of helping our clients reach their goal or potential, the company may not reach their highest level of achievement.

I remember once sensing an air of discontent among some of my team. It grew slowly and steadily, and at first, I tried to ignore the feeling that something was not right. Negative thoughts communicated through whispers by certain members of the team, filtered through the community; the staleness making it almost impossible to breathe. Clients seemed anxious and less positive or happy. Listening to my gut, I fired five of the negative team members— absolutely scared to death that the business would dissolve. On the contrary, fresh air filled the room. Clients smiled more. I found new team members whose guiding principles were aligned with mine– whose core values supported my business vision.

> ***Mini Morsel Sampling:***
>
> *Yes, products and services are the keys to a successful business but people are definitely a company's greatest asset! As the CEO of a company, a manager of a firm, a mother, a coach, a father, a small business owner or a student how do you grow your team? What core values do you have that will inspire them to succeed not just individually but as a team?*

Can we talk?

I just loved Joan Rivers. Sometimes she made me laugh till I cried. I always will remember her for her famous line "Can we talk?" She gossiped about events, fashion, headlines, even the rich and famous. And in listening to her, we all felt invited into her home, her world and her life. We all knew her courage in dealing with her husband's suicide and her plunge from fame to re-inventing herself and her art. She could be candid, she could be blunt, and she could tell it like it was. And we still loved and admired her. Because she was authentic.

I wish it were that simple to just sit down with people and talk. **Listen** to both sides where no one is right and no one is wrong—where we make conscious decisions to let go of our righteousness, our power, our own sense of what we think is honest, just, and decent.

In not sitting down and talking mindfully, we provide more fuel to our fires of impatience and indecision. Some of us find the answers in beliefs that satisfy our misguided longings, sometimes those values are chosen to hurt and destroy and we make vows that allow for a continued cycle of silence. We chose to stubbornly ignore each other's humanity and dignity. We do not allow time in our conversations to discover each other's gifts or talents which could really make a difference.

If we talked without being reactive, if we talked about our fears, dreams, values, and concerns, we would find we all want the same thing: love, peace, freedom and an unpolluted world not just environmentally but socio-economically. We want an unbiased political system. We want a world for our children and their children to thrive. But if we can't talk, listen, and give a little on both sides, we will remain in conflict; whether it is in our homes, schools, workplace, community, country, and the world.

Mini Morsel Sampling:

So can we talk? And if so, when? And at the end of our conversations, will we be willing to consciously resolve our differences? Thoughts?

Passion

I am a woman on fire! If you know me, you might say "Well, your astrological sign is Sagittarius, so you would have to be on fire."

However, I think that the fire within—the fire that burns and ignites my soul is my passion for things that move me forward. I believe that I have developed this passion over a long period. I would like to think that my enthusiasm for life, my zeal and appetite to try new things and experiment, brings me joy, energy, and an excitement for whatever comes next. I hope that passion also inspires others.

"Allow your passion to be your purpose and one day, it will become your profession."

"The most powerful weapon on earth is the human soul on fire."

I value my passion. It challenges me yet supports me even during tough times. My passion is not fueled by obsession or greed—traits that destroy what is noble and good. Instead, the fire within me operates from a deep desire to create a life of purpose.

Passion is magical; it opens doors for people. It helps us determine what is really important. It allows us a chance to give something back and make a difference. We can take a stand for the values of honesty, equality, kindness, and compassion; and change ourselves. This is not to say that obstacles or troubles do not occur, they do and will. However, my passion to endure, to overcome, and survive in spite of life's tragedies is paramount. My enthusiasm for endeavors of purpose outweighs the discouragement and life's negative circumstances. I have become more resilient.

Passion brings hope and joy to others. Surround yourself with passionate people and you cannot help but be passionate yourself. Be a woman or man on fire, you will experience your soul as the most powerful weapon on earth! Nurture your passion.

Mini Morsel Sampling:

What is your current passion? Where did it come from? Your values? If so, what are your values? Can your passion change, if so, why?

Recently, I had the opportunity to have lunch with a group of retired teachers I worked with during my days as a media specialist in the Bedford School District. It was a delightful time. We reminisced about the silly times we had and the agonizing days we experienced fueling the imaginations of our charges, instilling a love for learning and meeting the curricula requirements.

> "All labor that uplifts humanity has dignity and importance, and should be undertaken with painstaking excellence." ~ Martin Luther King Jr.

One thing that we all agreed upon is that we all worked so hard, but we took pleasure in our work. We felt passion and energetic each day because our labor uplifted others. It was dignified and important. Everything we did as teachers was undertaken with painstaking excellence, because that is what we expected from our students. We also helped each other and supported one another. We were always there for each other.

Our job wasn't a job. It was our passion.

When I think about celebrating Labor Day, I think about how many people hate their work. I believe that many of us change occupations thinking that the next employment opportunity will create the perfect work environment or the greatest opportunity for advancement. It is as if we are looking for that job where there will be no blood, sweat, and tears. We imagine a fantasy work environment as such, but in life, obstacles appear even at work—at every job.

How we approach our job shapes how we react to the difficulties and challenges that come with each profession. We can approach our careers with distaste, blaming others, standing on people's toes, pushing others aside, promoting ourselves as better than others **or** we can choose to uplift others, promote dignity in the workplace, share the importance of each other's contribution at work, and undertake each project with painstaking excellence. That is worthwhile labor that brings everyone joy and fulfillment even when times are difficult.

Mini Morsel Sampling:

How can you switch from a negative position about your career or job and create a positive mindset that will deliver successful and productive results? Try it. What do you notice?

First comes thought...

Everything begins with a thought. For example, when I was in college, I had to decide what kind career I wanted. I thought long and hard about it.

Based on my values, I made a conscious decision to choose teaching as a career. I felt like it allowed me to balance career with family. I also enjoy the creative side of teaching young people and encouraging critical thinking skills.

"First comes thought; then organization of that thought, into ideas and plans; then transformation of those plans into reality. The beginning, as you will observe, is in your imagination."

Thinking about teaching was not enough, however. I had to take very specific actions or steps to pursue my education and then find a school and department chair that would allow me to practice teach– a requirement for state certification. By doing this, I was transforming my plans into reality. I also imagined what it would be like to be a teacher. I imagined seeing myself in that position. And it came true.

But I didn't stop imagining. I continue each day envisioning what is possible. I realize that I do not have any limitations unless I believe that there are limits to what I am going to do. I believe in the power of my imagination. It is getting me to where I am going!

> ***Mini Morsel Sampling:***
>
> *Where is your imagination taking you? And will that lead you to your purpose?*
>
> *P.S. If you are not sure about where you are going, I can help you discover and uncover what your true purpose is! One of my workshops I invite you to attend is Discover You! It will be delivered online to a group of individuals willing to explore, expand, and evolve into you. Ask yourself:*

- *Are people telling you to go "find yourself?" How are you supposed to do that?*
- *Would you like to know who you really are and your purpose in life?*
- *"Why try to be someone you're not? Life is hard enough."*
- *Would you like a map that leads you to your true self? Then, it's time to discover you!*

Responsibility

It's not your fault...It is your responsibility

It is so easy to blame the things that go wrong rather than accept responsibility towards designing a healthy lifestyle. It's easy and maybe preferable to suggest that the food industry cannot be stopped from creating genetically modified foods. It's more comfortable to let others dictate the quantity of highly saturated foods filled with sugar, fat, and salt to grace our plates at home and in restaurants. It's funny how we don't know when to stop eating or why we overeat. It's interesting how we don't recognize tasty foods unless they are created by scientists and psychologists to consume artificial cuisines that

> "The more you take responsibility for your past and present, the more you are able to create the future you seek."

hardly nourishes and rarely sustains us. There are little nutrients in grocery products produced by food companies that are competing for high profit without any care for the health of our nation. Bring on the sugar coated doughnuts, the hamburger patty topped with cheese, sauces and more. Keep the soft drinks coming, create artificial water and call it a vitamin. Make the containers attractive and convince consumers that they are eating healthier. Convenience here is paramount. No one wants to plan, prepare, or cook meals anymore. It's just the way our lifestyle encourages us to live. The media plays advertisements enticing us to eat large while thinking small, an anomaly.

However, I want to suggest that it is our responsibility to take action. If you cannot go after lobbyists, start small. Create new habits in your own home to choose healthier foods. Read food labels. Ask members of your family to help plan, prepare, and cook meals. Reduce the amount of sugar you consume. Find ways to incorporate eating whole foods instead of junk. Don't bring the junk into the home or work place. Look for new recipes that are easy to prepare. Share them with family and friends. And when eating at restaurants, choose healthier dishes and smaller portions.

This is not about losing weight, although you may lose weight in the process. This is about taking responsibility for your own life and your health, because your health matters.

> ***Mini Morsel Sampling:***
>
> *It may not be your fault; but it is your responsibility to nourish your body. Are you up to the challenge? If so, what are you willing to do to make it happen?*

Make your influence positive

Remember, make your influence positive! Children see what you do but they also do what they see!

Recently, I viewed a video on you tube that was provocative. We know that young children imitate parent and adult behaviors.

But I observed in horror as I witnessed these behaviors. An adult screaming at a passerby and the young fellow alongside her yelling too; an adult riding an escalator smoking a cigarette as her young child holds her lit cigarette between her fingers.

I saw an adult impatiently waiting for the train—checking his watch and his child behind him pretending to irritably look at his watch; another adult angry at the ATM machine bashing it with her fists and her teenage daughter beating her knuckles at the neighboring automated teller.

I watched as a grown-up sprinted up the subway stairs banging into a woman's suitcase not offering to help pick up her belongings; his son followed suit.

I noticed another older person throw an empty soda can in the street and the tot behind mimicked that action. I heard adult temper tantrums only to be copied by the youngster nearby.

I watched again in sheer astonishment as an adult gave someone the finger and her child offered the same gesture.

What really shocked me the most was seeing a husband brutally abusing and beating his wife; and his son, without any hesitation participated in the violent action of his father.

It truly amazes me that we adults conduct ourselves inappropriately, disrespectfully, and without any sense of remorse or feeling for the other person. We react to situations without being aware that we are influencing others, especially our children.

What kind of role models have we become? We certainly are not the role models exhibiting acceptable behavior or reinforcing positive influence. Then what can we expect from our children if parents display behaviors like these? Why, then, do we wonder why we live in a society without ethics and morals? When we adults do what we want; children see what we do—and they will do what they see!

> ### *Mini Morsel Sampling:*
>
> *I challenge you to be a positive influence whether you are a parent, student, or employer! Whatever and whoever you are, you have the influence to demonstrate to our youth how to behave with respect. Email me and tell me what how you will do that.*

Time

There is always time or is there?

Do you put things off because you feel like there will be time later? You are not alone. I often say "There will be time—one day—when I finish this project, or complete this task." But recently, I have been more aware

> "Time is a gift that most of us take for granted."
> Cheryl Richardson

that my *one day* may not come. For example, I put much of my energy into my career. While that is noteworthy, I recognize that I am missing quality time with my friends and family. And, when I do spend time with them, it seems rushed. I realize that I need to bring balance back into my life. And, that is not easy. Balance can mean anything that is disharmonious in your life, career, money, friends and family, fun and recreation, physical environment, personal growth, romance or exercise and health.

As a former radio host on FTNS internet radio (What's Weighing You Down?), I interviewed Peter Ajello, a young man who thought he had time. In waiting for the right time, he almost lost his life. What was completely out of balance was his health. Peter weighed four hundred and five pounds, had uncontrolled diabetes, dangerously high cholesterol, and suffered from debilitating gout attacks in his legs. He could barely make it up a flight of stairs or around his block and wore a 5XL shirt and a size fifty-six pants around his waist. Peter Ajello was part of a growing group of Americans referred to as morbidly obese. Peter's complete turnaround and amazing transformation happened *just in time*.

Finding balance is difficult. I just want you to know that I struggle with it too. Nevertheless, I am incorporating some of the mental techniques and strategies to help me evolve into the person I am becoming. If you have areas in your life, where you want to improve your level of balance satisfaction, start creating new action plans to get to where you want to be. Just remember, time is of the essence.

Mini Morsel Sampling:

Are you struggling with time management issues? Do you seem to focus on just work or fun and not find time for that balance that restores us? Do you brush off friends and family because whatever you are doing now takes precedence? What is your action plan before time runs out?

"When will I get there?"

This question is one in which I have often asked myself.

The inquiry is often followed by the thought: "then this will happen."

I'll get my next raise or promotion. I will relax and make time for myself. I will invite friends over. I will volunteer for a cause I believe in. I will join a group.

Sometimes I think that when I get *there*, the event or experience will change my life. I will be different and I will feel different.

However, there have been times when I get *there*, that I am disappointed. There is an empty feeling and a longing to hurry on to the next place.

The process of getting there raises my anxiety level. What will I discover *there?* It probes me to find answers and to examine the **why** of getting somewhere.

Why do I need to get to the next destination, to rush to find what I think I need or want? Maybe I already have what I require.

Perhaps all I really need is to enjoy the process of going; wherever that place or situation may be.

As I look at arriving, perhaps I am already there; already where I need to be for the moment. Perhaps I have to keep arriving at various destinations and conditions in order to progress to a new stage in life.

I must remember to be in the moment, to relax, breathe, and be patient, to arrive when the time comes.

> ### *Mini Morsel Sampling:*
>
> *Where are you going? When will you get there? What will it look like? How can you be in the moment right now?*

There is a time for everything

- A time for birth and another for death,
- A time to plant and another to reap,
- A time to kill and another to heal,
- A time to destroy and another to construct,

- A time to cry and another to laugh,
- A time to lament and another to cheer,
- A time to make love and another to abstain,
- A time to embrace and another to part,
- A time to search and another to count your losses,
- A time to hold on and another to let go,
- A time to rip out and another to mend,
- A time to shut up and another to speak up,
- But there is always a time to make peace.

From time to time, I wonder what we are sowing and what we are reaping. I wonder how we are harvesting and what we are gathering.

Autumn is indeed the time of harvesting and of gathering together.

We can harvest love; we can gather together and provide each other with encouragement, comfort and support. We can sow the seeds of giving rather than receiving; forgiving rather than holding on to hate, envy and greed.

We can choose to be bountiful in the giving for one little seed that we plant yields much more than we need spreading across many boundaries. One little seed always produces a crop—maybe not right away, but in good time during the right season.

There is always a harvest and your season will come. Be patient: Plant, Sow, Harvest, and Gather.

> ***Mini Morsel Sampling:***
>
> *What are you planting? What kind of seeds? What are you harvesting? What are you planning to do with the fruit of your harvest?*

Attitude with Gratitude

In all things be mindfully thankful

I am reminded of a phrase from the Bible "in all things give thanks."

Thanking sometimes is just effortless. It is simple to give thanks when things are going our way, when life is good, when people are friendly, when the job or career is smoothly providing us with the accolades or the financial rewards that we deserve, when our families show unconditional love and even when the weather cooperates.

"Develop an attitude of gratitude, and give thanks to everything that happens to you, knowing that every step forward is a step towards achieving something bigger and better than your current situation."
Brian Tracy

It's hard to give thanks when financial burdens keep piling up.

It is much harder to give thanks when life takes a different turn. It's hard to give thanks when co-workers complain about our performance, or our boss chastised us for something that we felt was unfair. It's hard to give thanks when we didn't get the promotion we believed would be offered to us. It's hard to give thanks when our families fail or forsake us. It's hard to give thanks when even the weather turns foul and wicked.

However, when it is most difficult to give thanks, I say be mindful about thanking even in the hardest hours. We can choose to live in the past, the present, or the future. If we live in the past, we rehash all the things we should have, could have and ought to have done. It is almost impossible to be mindful about thanking, if we live with past mistakes or accomplishments. If we try to focus on our future—the tomorrows of our life, we tend to worry about what is coming our way. Again, it is difficult to offer thanks when we are stressing out or worrying about tomorrow.

So, I am suggesting that we focus on the present and give thanks in all things, being mindful about thanking. Choose a different perspective when burdens, obstacles, and even the weather make life hard. Be grateful for this very moment. You will not have it ever again. Be mindfully and thankfully present. Look at life and what the present obstacles are teaching you. Learn from them. There is an opportunity here, find it! There may even be a gift in this difficult hour.

It's not easy to be thankful when times are tough but it is not impossible. It just takes practice.

> ***Mini Morsel Sampling:***
>
> *Be mindfully thankful each day not only during the season of Thanksgiving or when things are perfect. If you practice being grateful, you will see the world differently. I guarantee you will enjoy the fruits and benefits of grateful living. Each day, say aloud what you are grateful for.*

Ready for a nor'easter!

Have you noticed that when weather people predict a major storm approaching, we scurry about to locate flashlights, candles, batteries, milk, bread, water and other staples? We secure the items to provide us with the comforts we need to survive, during a possible power outage, flood, snowstorm, or a state of emergency.

We purchase shovels, sand, salt, and other equipment to dig out or rescue our neighbors. We elicit the aid of contractors from other states just in case we need extra support. We even call in the National Guard at times!

Sometimes we anticipate the worst disaster because no one really knows what a storm will do to an area or the extent of the resulting damage. We can project outcomes but storms are erratic and can change direction in an instant. So we position sand bags, build barricades, and secure windows with plywood just in case we face a life-threatening scenario. Constant media coverage features forthcoming weather news, sensationalizing minute-by-minute potential changes. What might happen can cause great apprehension for people who need to re-adjust work schedules and alter school openings and closings.

Storms impact us greatly. We seek shelter, warmth and provisions to get us through several days of being cut off from the world. We stock up on medicines knowing fully well that transportation for several days might be impossible. We gear up to meet the storm full on!

Yet, as we face our own life storms, how do we prepare? We hide or at other times, we retreat. Many times, we find things to distract us like shopping, movies, drugs; anything to dull the senses.

However, we could brace for our own Nor'easter by soaring above it. We can recognize its arrival, yet we can fly above it. We can get ready by recruiting helpful resources, organizations, friends, family, neighbors, and self-help books. We can prepare because we know that deep down we have the answers; it may take a different flight plan or a pilot to help us discern our destination to find solutions. We may have to fly higher than what we are accustomed to; that can be very scary but also exciting! We can use the storms of life to motivate, inspire, and transport us to a new adventure if we will allow it.

My thought for you as you face your life storms is to be like the eagle, be courageous and soar above the tempests. Find new ways to respond to your upheavals. You may actually find that you love the ascent.

Mini Morsel Sampling:

I would love it if you to share what upheavals you encounter and what resources you are employing that gets you moving forward.

The "I Choose" Commitment!

"It was by chance, you say that this circumstance materialized." But I say, you chose. You envisioned, you imagined, and it materialized. You could see it, taste it, feel it, hear it, and intuitively sense its arrival. You chose—consciously or subconsciously. Your thoughts became things.

We choose how we perform! We often make excuses for our actions. We are right and everyone else is wrong. It's quick and mindless to justify our acts. Point the finger, lay blame on a co-worker, and turn against a friend. It's not easy to make changes to improve our conduct, to deviate from quick word preferences or to bear responsibility for our substandard behavior patterns. But when we do decide to, we can choose to replace our deportment with moral endeavors; it's not by chance or accident that we change. We choose. Thus begins the process of discovering our true self, from which we gain meaning every moment in our day.

I love feeling self-motivated. But there are days that I feel manipulated, depleted and abused; so it is harder to find purpose and get re-focused. But once I choose to inspire myself, I no longer feel controlled. I am in charge and encouraged!

I relish being part of a community where I believe I am making a difference, being useful and not exploited. But I choose that belief; no one has to convince me or tell me. I just know it.

I am finally learning to listen to my inner voice; be still a little longer in order to understand, notice, and appreciate what is essential in life. I no longer listen so intently to the random opinions of others because judgment is subjective. I choose an inner confidence from which I operate!

I also prefer excellence instead of mediocrity. I want to shine at both work and home; that is just my personality. But I do not feel the need to compete against others to win a prize, to be congratulated or to earn admiration. I choose to excel in helping others be their noblest. I choose an inward sense of gratification that the job I did was worthy.

I could certainly hold a pity party for myself on most days of the week. Yet, I consciously choose to build myself up and not tear myself down. That kind of negativity gets me nowhere.

I wonder if you will stand with me and pledge to the "I Choose" commitment. Choose choice, make changes, be motivated, useful and excel. Choose self-esteem, building others' self-worth as you do yours; and above all, take moments during the day to choose to listen to your inner voice. You may be pleasantly surprised at what it will tell you.

Mini Morsel Sampling:

Choosing is just an attitude change; but it has to be intentionally revisited throughout the day. Let me know what you are choosing or if you need help discovering how or what to choose!

I have always tried to be a positive person. Sometimes people think I am living in a glass bottle. They think I am living in a dream world and not in reality. My life is just like yours—some days are great, some days are not so great; and some days are an utter disaster. I have had my highs and lows, my times of tremendous joy and ultimate despair. I have suffered grave illnesses, depression, and even neared death. I have watched family members die slowly from disease. I have seen young people close to me enter the world of drugs and mental illness.

> "The most vital thing in a man's life is his mental attitude."

How do I cope? My resiliency comes from my positive attitude. First, I am thankful. I am grateful for the things I have. Second, I choose to look at a brighter picture because in reality, if I choose to look at life as a horrible place, my thoughts will spiral downward and I will attract more negativity.

And, if I believe that my health is vital to my well-being, then I need to focus on the thing most important to my good health; and that is my mental attitude.

I choose to think of my life as abundant with struggles; but I am learning to see new possibilities out of the difficult moments. I am allowing and accepting all the gifts of life that are coming my way.

> ***Mini Morsel Sampling:***
>
> *Where is your mental attitude these days? What are you consciously choosing—positive or negative thoughts?*

Hidden Blessings

Do you see your difficulties as an overwhelming curse? Do you wish your hardships would simply disappear? Do your misfortunes shake your beliefs, hopes and dreams? Do you harbor doubt, fear, anger, and resentment because of your current life story?

The more I talk with people, the more I recognize that we share the same burdens, troubles, and pain. We all face loss, disappointment, regret, rejection and frustration; it's just a part of life.

What if we didn't feel fear or pain or undergo setbacks, and failures? Some of us might think that would be fantastic. But I believe that if we did not encounter whatever trial we were given at whatever point in our lifetime, we might have not spotted the hidden blessings that often appear when we least expect it.

For example, if I did not understand fear, I would have not developed self-confidence. If I did not doubt and know failure, I would not recognize belief and accomplishment. If I did not suffer loss, I would not understand how to counsel or comfort someone in bereavement. If I did not know illness, I would not be able to comprehend the physical or mental diseases many of us confront. If I did not know sorrow, I would not appreciate joy. If I did not face rejection, I would not know how to accept others who are often tossed aside, ignored or abused. If I did not know unkindness, I would not feel compassion and empathy. If I did not know injustice, I would not know how to be impartial and fair. If I did not experience jealously, I would have not been capable of trust. If I did not know vindictiveness, I would not know how to understand mercy and forgiveness. If I did not know weakness, I would not have learned strength and resilience.

And if I did not know hatred, I would not know how to love unconditionally.

So, out of these tribulations, I discovered hidden healing messages and blessings. I saw the why of my angst and I am grateful.

There are opportunities for you to grow and gather meaning in the midst of turbulence. The hardships you may face are grooming you to love, be patient, kind and compassionate. They are teaching you to forgive and to welcome the unwanted and displaced.

Mini Morsel Sampling:

What are your hardships telling you? How are they changing you? What are the hidden blessings? I would love to know what you learn from these life events and how you are choosing to use your blessings as opportunities and gifts.

The real to do list: Be present

I think most of us are asking, "Is it spring already?" Winter has been brutally harsh. We are longing for the smell of freshly cut grass, the sound of animals awakening from their sleep and blending their voices in harmony.

As we now march into springtime, I wonder what that will mean for our to-do lists. There will be additional yard work, weeding, mowing. There may even be seeds to plant and outside furniture to clean.

If you are like me, I make my weekly and daily lists and cross off the chores/projects that I have completed. But my responsibilities appear endless. I seem to add more and more tasks to my personal and work calendar. It seems like I rarely have the time to socialize and to be in the moment. Yet, each day I realize how important it is to be present.

To laugh at the little things and even the annoyances because that is all they are—temporary nuisances.

To sing with abandon with friends or alone, (without being on key) just for fun.

To read under a tree or in the backyard. Wherever you can quietly travel between the pages and lose yourself to the discovery of new places, people, or events.

To count your blessings even when a disaster strikes because we are all blessed in so many ways.

Never lose sight that faith is our anchor that grounds us to remain strong and resilient.

Hug your little ones—your children, grandchildren, and pets. Even grownups like hugs. Embrace and nurture your friends and family. You may lift someone's spirit and in the process and uplift yourself.

Walk barefoot in the grass. While this may not be possible for all of us to do, I would like to say walk somewhere barefoot. Experience the softness of the carpet, the coldness of the ceramic tile, the hardness of the pebbles on the beach. Give thanks and be grateful, eventually you will experience happiness. Appreciate everything you are given each day—the good, the bad, and the ugly.

Love without conditions. Recognize the imperfections in each of us, and bring unconditional love to each relationship.

And then, keep on loving for that is all we need—love.

Take deep breaths when life becomes overwhelming or stressful, just breathe!

Mini Morsel Sampling:

Dive into your passion today. Be present in the moment. Your personal and work projects are important but more important is focusing on the now; so jump in!

Are you defeated or present?

Recently, I attended my weekly yoga class. It is a precious time for me since I seem to rush through life, rarely feeling like I am breathing. So this particular evening, my talented and ever-observant teacher worked on each person's posture. I was called to the front of the room and asked to stand sideways. My teacher expertly changed the direction of my pelvis and helped me lift my chest in such a way that my ears lined up to my shoulders. I felt suspended in the air, relaxed and in control. But there was something more noticeable in my demeanor.

Interestingly enough, one of my classmates remarked that when I first came to the front of the room, I looked defeated but now I looked present. The comment was made by someone who doesn't know me well but she certainly read my body language correctly. Her observation made me realize how often we are perceived as defeated and how we could choose to be seen as present.

Are you longing to be in the *here and now* and not in the past or the future?

Our body language says a lot about our internal feelings and emotions. We physically express joy, anger, sadness, rejection, loneliness, excitement, despair and defeat in the way that we hold our head, shoulders, back and even our eyes

We encounter regular defeats (or what we perceive as defeats). It is how we hold ourselves together that helps us cope with the obstacle. We can choose to hold our bodies in a posture that screams defeat or we can stand tall and tackle the challenge head-on.

We can offer a smile, a hug, an email of encouragement, a prayer, a gentle ear or a full loving heart. During your defeat or your setback, you are just gathering new information—compassion and loving kindness. If you are present in the moment and bring others into the present, defeat is not an option. Defeat is a challenge, but if you stand strong with self-worth, you will not be overpowered! You will be victorious!

> ### *Mini Morsel Sampling:*
>
> *Remember we all feel defeated at times. You are not alone. This defeated feeling is a temporary setback or a moment in time. This feeling of defeat does not define who you are or who you will become. This defeated feeling is a teachable moment where you can take away a lesson. When you feel defeated, you will do this...Step out of yourself. Stop focusing on you; think of others. Do something for someone. Don't stress about not being perfect. It's OK to be imperfect; you are human. Remember that today is a gift no matter how empty the inside of the box. Resist complaining and instead be grateful. Make a change; small adjustments along the way keep you moving forward.*

Your Very Own Mac 'n Cheese Fixings for Positive Performance

There is no secret recipe for Mac 'n Cheese. You can use whatever cheese or macaroni you want. You can top your recipe with or without breadcrumbs. You can make it one way one day and change the flavorings to suit your tastes. The most important thing to remember: it takes **practice** to craft your own version of this dish. It takes repetition and **patience**. It takes **mindful attention** down to the smallest detail even to the oven temperature and cooking time. Remember performing or executing the process repeatedly doesn't make for a perfect outcome! But hopefully you learned a **lesson** from your accomplishment. Next time, after conscious **attention** and practice, your version will be tastier.

So it is with positive **performance**. You strive to perform in ways that yield optimistic results. You want to perform better at home, work, and play. You want to create a more optimistic **outlook** reducing the amount of negativity that comes your way. You want a more balanced life. You want lasting relationships, a more rewarding career, and to be seen as a winner. And, when you fail, make a mistake, or find an obstacle pushing you away from your desire, the result feels disastrous. The little negative voice in your head reprimands you and beats you down. You let that voice rule your life and write your script until you memorize it line by line. You believe that screenplay as truth. You become what you **believe**. You tell yourself "Nothing goes well for me." "I am a loser." "I can't do it." "I'll never be a success at anything."

Instead of exploring new ways of seeing your **mistakes** and beliefs as **opportunities**, you stay stuck in that negative state. Instead of expanding your horizons and experimenting, you fear the consequences. In that **mindset**, you will not evolve as a **positive performer**.

Living life as a recipe with exact ingredients does not always produce flawless results. It is only possible with daily **mental practice** and an **attitude readjustment**. It takes looking at life from a new **perspective**. Like Robin Williams said "You will have bad times, but they will always wake you up to the stuff you weren't paying attention to."

And, often, it is the wakeup call we need. We just have to spice up the **behavior** to enhance performance flavor.

What can you do then to season your mac 'n cheese life recipe and perform more positively? Here are some simple practices:

1. Start each day with a **positive affirmation**. Say aloud "Today is a good day for me. I am going to close this deal at work. I am going to be more patient with the children. I am going to be the best I can be today at my tennis game. Today, I will learn from the mistakes I make at work, at school, at home."

2. Each morning as you dress for work, walk to the train, or drive in your car focus on embracing an **attitude of gratitude.** Be grateful and mean it. Find the small and large things that lift your soul and make you appreciative of what you have **now**. Find at least one thing a day you are grateful for and write it in a notebook or on your calendar.

3. Often we get excited when we reach our big aspirations. But what about the small goals? The bite-size accomplishments are yours to celebrate not to lament over. It's the little achievements that will make your mac 'n cheese dish delectable. Delight in your **mini morsels**.

4. How many times have we had to wait in line at a store, wait in traffic on a highway, or wait to hear if something we have done will be accepted? How do we manage the wait? Are we grumpy, impatient, angry, and moody? Do we scream and throw a tantrum? Or do we look at the **benefits** for the time you have to do something **positive**, productive, and different? We can let all the little things throw us or we can **choose** to let the inconveniences provide us with a **new perspective** of the situation.

5. Life can be **tough** at times. We make mistakes. We are thrown curve balls expectantly. We inadvertently say the wrong things. We act clumsy; forget someone's name or birthday. We appear distracted. We'd like things to go our way, but they don't. In all the awkward and unpleasant situations, fill it with **humor**. Be willing to act foolish or funny or crack a joke. After all, we are human. It is our nature to forget, be impatient, or act self-conscious. Laughing at ourselves releases the tension of the moment. Robin Williams said "Comedy can be a cathartic way to deal with personal trauma." Liberate yourself with **laughter**. Let it be a therapeutic healer.

6. Bring on the **mistakes.** But don't let the things you did wrong define who you are. Instead, focus

on what went wrong, why it happened, and how not to repeat the same errors going forward. These lessons learned provide **opportunities** for **growth**.

7. Tell negative Nelly or Neil to take a hike. When she or he pops into your head and whispers in your ear "You're not good enough," **rephrase** the pessimistic statement into a positive one. Be **confident**. Tell yourself "I am good enough!"

8. Stay in the **present** moment. Yesterday is gone. Tomorrow is not here. This moment is where you are now. Let the present seem like you only have **now**. It will never be again. Treasure **each moment** whether it is good, bad, or ugly. There is some beauty in it all. Let stuff that happened even a few minutes ago stay in the past. Let what you hope for in the future not consume you with anxiety. It is not here yet. All you have is this **literal instant**.

9. Surround yourself with positive people, situations, and teammates. People who are negative are like toxic waste and give off poisonous fumes. Consorting with negative friends and family shift you from the confident human being you are **becoming**. If you breathe in their lethal self-talk, you will be surprised how

quickly you will sound like them. Be an encouraging light for others and let others be a **constructive light** for you.

Marilyn, PsyD

The Positive Performance Life Coach and Applied Sports Psychologist

Email: drm@drmlifecoach.com
Website: www.drmlifecoach.weebly.com
Phone: 203-979-0269

ROOM FOR DESSERT?

A Mac 'N Cheese Acronym

BE

Mindfully Present

Act Responsibly

Carefully practice your intentions

Nurture & adjust your perspective

Choose attitude with gratitude

Harvest positivity

Enthusiastically Encourage

Envision the possibilities

Stay in the present moment; learn from your mistakes

Evolve into a positive performer!

Urgent Plea!

Thank You For Reading My Book!

I really appreciate all of your feedback, and I love hearing what you have to say.

I need your input to make the next version of this book and my future books even better.

Please leave me a helpful review on Amazon letting me know what you thought of the book.

Thank you so much!

Thank you so much!
~ Marilyn Gansel, PsyD